What is Environmental Sociology?

What is Sociology? Series

What is Environmental Sociology?

DIANA STUART

polity

First published in 2021 by Polity Press

Polity Press
65 Bridge Street
Cambridge CB2 1UR, UK

Polity Press
101 Station Landing
Suite 300
Medford, MA 02155, USA

ISBN-13: 978-1-5095-4438-7
ISBN-13: 978-1-5095-4439-4 (pb)

A catalogue record for this book is available from the British Library.

Library of Congress Cataloging-in-Publication Data
Names: Stuart, Diana (Diana Lynne), 1979- author.
Title: What is environmental sociology? / Diana Stuart.
Description: Medford : Polity Press, 2021. | Series: What is sociology? |
   Includes bibliographical references and index. | Summary: "A succinct
   primer on how to think critically about society/environment
   interactions"-- Provided by publisher.
Identifiers: LCCN 2021000067 (print) | LCCN 2021000068 (ebook) | ISBN
   9781509544387 (hardback) | ISBN 9781509544394 (paperback) | ISBN
   9781509544400 (epub)
Subjects: LCSH: Environmental sociology.
Classification: LCC GE195 .S7858 2021 (print) | LCC GE195 (ebook) | DDC
   304.2--dc23
LC record available at https://lccn.loc.gov/2021000067
LC ebook record available at https://lccn.loc.gov/2021000068

Typeset in 10.5 on 12pt Sabon
by Fakenham Prepress Solutions, Fakenham, Norfolk NR21 8NL
Printed and bound in the UK by CPI Group (UK) Ltd, Croydon

For further information on Polity, visit our website:
politybooks.com

Contents

Preface

My approach for this book was inspired by my experiences teaching undergraduate and graduate-level environmental sociology and environmental studies courses over the past ten years. In recent years, I have noticed a significant shift in student morale. The existential environmental threats we currently face, especially those posed by climate change, are impossible for students to ignore, and many feel powerless and defeated by the lack of meaningful action taken. In my courses, I actively work to counter these feelings, as they only help to ensure our current trajectory. I emphasize potential solutions and alternative pathways. I also find it critical to repeatedly communicate and illustrate that another way and a different future is possible. We are not simply "doomed," as there are many paths left to choose from, some that offer much more positive social and ecological outcomes than others.

There is tremendous work to be done to correct our current trajectory and steer a course toward the best future possible. Even if this path is through uncharted waters and the challenges are daunting, there is a moral imperative to keep going. We are also in an exciting moment in history, where public opinions have shifted and social movements are challenging the current system. At the same time, powerful groups are using vast financial resources to protect the status quo. In addition, unexpected events, like the Covid-19 pandemic, can quickly reshape what is politically and socially possible. Rather than feeling powerless and dreading the inevitable environmental disasters ahead, it remains critical that we keep working to justly minimize harm. Environmental sociologists continue to play a key role in this work. In this book, I highlight this work and focus on how environmental sociology can help us to address the escalating environmental threats we face and forge pathways for the best possible future.

1
Environmental Sociology: In Uncharted Waters

Environmental sociology is a subdiscipline of sociology that examines the relationships between humans and the entities and processes on Earth that are often lumped together and referred to as "nature" or "the environment." Dominant philosophical views from the past fortified the use of such terms to refer to what lies outside of the human or social world. In other words, we humans are *here* in society and "nature" or "the environment" is somewhere else, *out there*. However, as scientists, philosophers, environmentalists, and many others increasingly have realized, the idea of a separation between nature and society is far from accurate. We must also acknowledge that both "nature" and "society" represent complicated configurations of beings and entities and are concepts that are diverse, complex, and socially constructed.

If there is something called "the environment," then we live in it, depend on it, and are a part of it. It is where we live, work, and recreate. It includes all life, plant and animal, as well as nonliving things such as soil, rocks, water, and atmosphere. While some who want to protect "the environment" might be thinking only about the nonhuman world, our inherent relationships and dependencies make humans a part of the biophysical community. The idea of a divide between nature and society has perniciously masked these fundamental linkages. The belief that we can take resources from "the environment" and put waste into "the environment" without any consequences is not only false, but dangerous. The long-ignored interconnections between the human and nonhuman worlds are now clear, as environmental impacts directly affecting humans have increased over time. In response to these impacts, environmental sociology emerged in the 1970s to better understand these overlooked relationships.

While environmental sociology emerged over forty years ago, this book focuses on more recent definitions and applications. Gould and Lewis (2009: 2) define environmental sociology as "the study of how social systems interact with ecosystems." Lockie (2015: 140) defines environmental sociology as "the application of our sociological imaginations to the connections among people, institutions, technologies and ecosystems that make society possible." In both of these definitions is the term *ecosystem*, which refers to all living organisms in a community, the nonliving components of this community, and their relationships. While humans affect ecosystems and ecosystems affect humans, a more accurate depiction is that humans *depend* on ecosystems, live in ecosystems, and are also driving rapid ecosystem change. With accelerating climate change and biodiversity loss, it has become clear that human activities now shape the fate of all species on the planet. Therefore, as a field of study, environmental sociology examines how humans interact with the nonhuman beings, entities, and processes on Earth and how these relationships shape our *mutual* existence, survival, and possibilities for flourishing.

In Uncharted Waters

As we now face global and existential environmental threats, environmental sociology has never been more important. Early environmental issues such as the pollution in the Cuyahoga River and Love Canal were regional. While we still face these kinds of environmental issues, which threaten humans and other species in certain places, we now also face environmental crises that are *existential* because they threaten the future existence of our species and others. Environmental issues have been on the social radar for decades, yet we have reached a new era of global and existential environmental threats. Calling these threats "existential" may sound extreme or exaggerated, but unfortunately it is not. We face unprecedented global environmental impacts putting our existence at risk. In recent reports from the Intergovernmental Panel on Climate Change (IPCC 2018) and the Intergovernmental Science-Policy Platform on Biodiversity and Ecosystem Services (IPBES 2019), scientists have illustrated the severity of both the climate and biodiversity crises and how current trajectories put us at risk of societal collapse, massive population loss, and even possible extinction. These reports call for rapid and unprecedented changes in *all* aspects of society to address these crises and minimize ecological and social impacts. The climate and biodiversity crises together pose a global existential threat to the human race. While these two distinct crises are discussed here, they will sometimes be grouped together and referred to as "the environmental crisis" or "existential threats" throughout the book.

With only about a 1.1° Celsius (C) average global temperature increase thus far, we are already seeing serious impacts due to global climate change, including unprecedented fires, floods, and hurricanes; and much more severe impacts are projected as warming continues. The words "crisis" and "emergency" are increasingly used by scientists and in the media to describe climate change. Steffen and colleagues (2018) explain the very real possibility of reaching a critical threshold of warming, a global tipping point, after which additional warming would be uncontrollable, resulting in a "Hothouse Earth" scenario. In *Nature*, Lenton and colleagues (2019: 595) state that climate change "is an existential threat to civilization," explaining that "the evidence from tipping points alone suggests that we are in a state of planetary emergency." Finally, Ripple and colleagues (2019: 1), representing the Alliance of World Scientists, identify "disturbing" and "worrisome" vital signs that they state "clearly and unequivocally" illustrate we are in a "climate emergency." Klinenberg et al. (2020: 664) and other sociologists argue that climate change needs to be a central focus in all subdisciplines of sociology, as it is rapidly transforming the conditions of life on the planet for all people and "everything is at stake."

Although the climate crisis contributes to biodiversity loss, the biodiversity crisis is considered a separate yet related crisis. Biodiversity loss receives much less public attention than climate change, yet it too poses an existential threat to humans. Imagine the impacts on humans if extinction cascades resulted in the loss of insect pollination or the loss of all ocean life. This is why terms like "ecological crisis" and "biodiversity crisis" are now commonly used by scientists and in the media. For example, a letter representing almost 100 scientists was published in October of 2018 titled: "Facts about our ecological crisis are incontrovertible" (Green and Scott Cato 2018). A year later, the United Nations report on biodiversity and ecosystem services (IPBES 2019) resulted in scientists publicly calling for rapid funding and intervention to address the "biodiversity crisis" (Malcom et al. 2019). The IPBES media release (2019) states that species loss has accelerated to rates that "constitute a direct threat to human well-being in all regions of the world." The climate and biodiversity crises can both be seen as "crises of civilization" that together represent an unprecedented existential threat.

The climate and biodiversity crises are related, as climate change increases extinction rates, but they are also related in how the impacts of these crises are unfolding, who is most affected, the underlying drivers, and the likely solutions. Environmental sociology can play a critical role in understanding these impacts, drivers, and solutions. Already, environmental sociologists are working to identify unequal and unjust impacts, root drivers of impacts that are overlooked by oversimplified diagnoses, the ineffectiveness and inadequacy of proposed solutions, and the extent of social transformation necessary to stave off these existential threats. While this book will draw from examples beyond these global crises, it will emphasize how current and future environmental sociologists can contribute to understanding and addressing these escalating threats. We are in uncharted waters, and environmental sociologists can play an important role identifying and advocating for the most effective and just paths forward.

While crises create uncertain and daunting times, they also can create opportunities for change that can be positive. Having plans for positive social transformation already formulated is critical for being prepared to direct the path of change. It is those who have studied and who understand the impacts and drivers of problems who can point us in the direction of effective and just solutions. Conditions can rapidly change due to environmental, economic, and health crises (e.g., the Covid-19 pandemic) and ideas that were previously deemed unfeasible can suddenly gain popular support. As windows open for positive social change, environmental sociologists can play a key role in identifying effective solutions and helping to steer society toward paths that increase social and ecological well-being. This important work requires a thorough understanding of the complex relationships between nature and society.

Navigating Nature and Society

Navigating the study of nature and society is a relatively recent endeavor, due to philosophical and scientific paradigms that remained dominant for hundreds of years. The Enlightenment period, between the seventeenth and nineteenth centuries, was also called the Age of Reason, as scholars emphasized how humans can use their unique intellectual abilities to control and dominate nature for social progress. Nature was regarded as separate from and subordinate to humans, reinforcing the notion of human exceptionalism. This rationality also influenced the development of the sciences into distinctive and isolated disciplines for examining the social and natural worlds. Sociology developed specifically as a science of society, using social facts to explain social phenomena. Yet, as with many other disciplines, over time scholars increasingly realized that separating nature and society was a false and dangerous depiction of the world.

Environmental sociology emerged in the 1970s as a result of calls for new theories and methods that cast away Enlightenment notions of society as separate from nature, offering a more holistic (and realistic) understanding of the world. In a series of articles, Dunlap and Catton convincingly argued for a new kind of sociology involving a paradigmatic and methodological shift away from a solely anthropogenic focus (Catton and Dunlap 1978a, 1978b, 1980; Dunlap and Catton 1979, 1983). They called for a purposeful move away from the dominant human exceptionalism perspective in sociology toward one that incorporates ecological entities and processes. It has been over forty years since these articles were published, and a diverse body of scholarship has emerged in environmental sociology.

It is important to know that sociology was not the only or first discipline to breach the nature-society divide. Human geographers were examining the relationships between people, place, and the environment long before environmental sociology existed. Anthropologists were also examining how people lived and related to their surroundings. In addition, human ecology, a subfield related to multiple disciplines, focused on relationships between humans and the biophysical world. In the past few decades, new areas of study have also emerged that cross the nature-society divide. Political ecology, a subdiscipline in geography, examines nature-society relations, focusing on power, marginalization, and political economy. Ecologists have also developed approaches to study the resilience of social-ecological systems. In summary, as the nature-society divide has been increasingly deemed false, scholars in a range of disciplines have developed new theories and approaches to examine nature and society together.

What are theories? Theories are general explanations of how the world works or how processes unfold. For example, the theory of evolution explains how over time life evolved into diverse and specialized species across the globe. The theory of inheritance explains how the traits from one generation are passed on to the next. These are theories that have stood the test of time and are still widely believed to explain reality accurately. Other theories, however, have been found to be false and were replaced by others. For example, the flat earth theory was deemed false and superseded by the round earth theory. Maternal impression theory, which explained birth defects as a product of the pregnant mother's thoughts, was also found to be false and replaced by genetic theory. Some theories offer explanations that hold, while others are eventually debunked, replaced, and disregarded. Theories are useful for multiple reasons: they can guide research questions, they can help to reveal specific patterns, and they can foster broader discussions that many scholars can contribute to over time.

In sociology, theories explain how society functions or how people act and relate to each other. Some theories explain how society works at a macro scale and focus on how the structures of social institutions, policies, and economic systems shape society. For example, Marxist theory posits that the mode of production, or how our economy is organized, creates a social order that results in specific class relations, power dynamics, and social and environmental outcomes. Other theories focus on individuals or groups of people and how they behave or interact with each other. For many years, social scientists debated whether it is the structure of our social order or choice and individual agency that most influence human behavior. Most scholars now agree that both are very important and that they are in many ways related. The ideas, beliefs, and choices of individuals are shaped and reinforced by the social order; and the ideas, beliefs, and actions of individuals are critical to either maintain or alter the social order.

While many theories from sociology have been applied or adapted to study the environment, new theories have also emerged specifically to examine nature-society relations. For example, the treadmill-of-production theory (Schnaiberg 1980), which will be further explained in Chapter 3, describes how increasing levels of production result in both more withdrawals from the environment and more additions into the environment, increasing levels of environmental degradation. Another example is ecological modernization theory, which will be discussed in more depth in Chapter 4. This theory explains how we can solve environmental problems using science, markets, and policy reforms to reshape relations in ways that adequately address environmental degradation and support economic growth (Mol and Spaargaren 2000). You may have noticed that these two theories are not complementary. These contrasting theories and related debates will be further examined in later chapters, as they continue to shape not only our understanding of the drivers of environmental impacts but also what solutions we should pursue.

A variety of different social science methods are used in environmental sociology. These include both quantitative and qualitative methods. Quantitative studies include examining survey and public opinion data to better understand attitudes, values, and beliefs. Surveys are also useful to understand behaviors. In addition, quantitative studies have looked at both social and biophysical data together to better understand correlations, drivers, and impacts. Quantitative work usually involves large data sets and statistical analysis, and has been used in some cases to test different social theories. Qualitative work in environmental sociology includes discourse or policy analysis, focus groups, and personal interviews to examine framing, influences, rationales, and justifications. While quantitative analysis might be better suited to understand *what* is happening and *to what extent,* as well as opinions, attitudes, and correlations, qualitative work is often needed to understand *why* people do or think what they do, and to expose influences that might otherwise be overlooked. Many publications in environmental sociology also focus on applications of theory to specific environmental issues; they may not use any primary data. All of this work contributes to a more comprehensive understanding of the impacts on, drivers of, and solutions to environmental issues. Throughout the book, specific studies will be highlighted along with the methods used to illustrate the range of research conducted.

It should also be noted that while rural sociology and the sociology of natural resources developed distinctively from environmental sociology, the differences in theory, approach, problems, and institutions define these subdisciplines rather than the locations and topics of case studies (Buttel 2000). Rural sociology has a long history of studying the relationships between people and rural places, including examining agriculture, recreation, and natural resources. While distinctive frameworks and theories initially guided rural sociology, increasingly theory and approaches from environmental sociology have also been applied to case studies. This makes the distinction between rural and environmental sociology increasingly blurry, but in a way that likely benefits scholars associated with each subdiscipline. Just because a case study is in a rural location or focuses on agriculture does not mean that theories from environmental sociology cannot be applied. In fact, an increasing number of scholars have demonstrated the benefits of such applications (e.g., Ipsen 2016, Houser et al. 2017, Ternes 2019). Similarly, approaches from environmental sociology can be applied to studies that might be topically more associated with other subdisciplines. This includes science and technology studies (e.g., Lidskog and Sundqvist 2018), urban studies (e.g., Scanu 2015), migration (e.g., Ransan-Cooper 2016), and development (e.g., Givens et al. 2016, Westoby and Lyons 2016). Overall, the approaches from environmental sociology can be applied much more widely than the topics that were originally the focus of the subdiscipline. These approaches are also increasingly important in interdisciplinary work. There is growing recognition of the benefits of not only crossing the nature-society divide but also of being open to using theories, frameworks, and approaches from a variety of different social and natural science disciplines. As a result, interdisciplinary projects have received increasing levels of funding over the past few decades and will continue to be a vital part of environmental research. As we face escalating existential threats, the theories and methods used by environmental sociologists will be vital to interdisciplinary efforts to understand and address our environmental crisis.

Public Environmental Sociology in an Age of Crisis

Increasingly, environmental sociologists are participating in cutting-edge research and are publishing work with important social implications. Their research has illustrated how environmental impacts are unequally experienced, and elucidated the overlooked relationships between economic and environmental realities, the false promises of "silver bullet" environmental solutions, and how we can find environmental solutions that are the most effective and just. This work is not only published in prominent academic journals but is also highlighted in mainstream media outlets such as the *New York Times*. As we are in uncharted waters, facing increasing existential threats, this work is more important than ever.

This book introduces environmental sociology through focusing on recent work in the field and also through emphasizing *public sociology*. Public sociology goes beyond sociology for academic purposes and involves research that has important implications for society. For example, work highlighted in this book has important implications for identifying, understanding, and addressing our escalating environmental crisis, which is of increasing public concern. Public sociology can result in findings that garner widespread attention and are useful to policymakers, social movements, and others working to foster positive social change. Environmental sociologists continue to make significant contributions to public sociology, and diverse examples of public sociology will be emphasized throughout the book. While most of the examples and approaches in this book focus on scholars from the United States (US) and Europe, there is important work in environmental sociology happening across the globe and in the Global South, some of which will be highlighted in this book. The primary focus on the Global North is due to the accelerating levels of overproduction and overconsumption in affluent nations that are primary drivers of our environmental crisis and therefore must be addressed.

In an age of increasing and intersecting crises—not only related to climate change and biodiversity loss but also economic inequality, health, democracy, and institutionalized racism—it is easy to become overwhelmed and disillusioned by any one of the crises we face. For some it may seem more comforting to deny that these crises exist. Others may choose the path of optimism, believing that everything will work out fine in the end because technology or human innovation will save us from the worst possible outcomes. In addition, there are those who have already decided that the fate of humanity is sealed, we are doomed, all hope is lost, and there is nothing we can do about it. These are narratives that people often tell themselves because, according to each of these narratives, we should simply continue with the status quo. These responses are understandable, as social change is difficult to imagine and it is easy to feel overwhelmed and helpless when faced with multiple and escalating crises. However, these narratives represent forms of delusion that distract us from the real work that needs to be done. Both falsely optimistic and fatalistic narratives can serve as pernicious distractions that delay the necessary action. We stand at a critical moment in time where there is still a small window of opportunity to act to prevent the worst-case scenarios. Indeed, the impacts are very serious and some are already unavoidable. For example, average global temperatures will continue to increase; however, the extent of this increase is yet to be determined. As Rebecca Elliott (2018) explains, climate change has and will continue to result in material, psychological, and emotional loss. Some loss is inevitable, yet a 2°C warmer future and a 4°C warmer future by 2100 will be dramatically different, with vast moral implications. None of the crises we face represent an "all or nothing" situation that would support giving up. In each case, we can either do very little and experience tremendous loss, or we can do as much as we can to create the most sustainable and just future possible. Therefore, public environmental sociology takes on critical importance in this crucial moment. It is not a time to take comfort in false narratives. It is a time to understand what is at stake and to go *all in*. As we will see throughout this book, public environmental sociology has and will continue to play an important role in this work.

Book Overview

In the following chapters, we will examine the topics, theories, and approaches that embody environmental sociology and illustrate specific contributions to understanding the social dimensions of environmental impacts, the drivers of environmental impacts, and possible solutions. Recent work will be emphasized, yet some classic studies will also be discussed. Throughout the book, we will continue to focus on the existential environmental crisis that we face related to climate change and biodiversity loss. This crisis is very real, and the risks are so great that for some of us it is difficult to think about anything else. In this book, the reality of these threats will be consistently acknowledged—as well as the moral implications of our choices moving forward. In this time of crisis, we cannot shy away from questions of morality. This focus is not intended to induce fear. It is meant to be truthful, as knowing the truth is necessary to act most effectively to minimize the impacts ahead. In addition to these existential threats, we will also examine a range of other environmental topics, including toxins, health, and environmental justice, as well as diverse examples of methodologies and public sociology.

Chapter 2 focuses on the social dimensions of environmental impacts, or the ways in which impacts are identified, perceived, framed, and communicated. It covers the contested interpretations of science, risk perception, social constructionist perspectives, as well as environmental justice. Environmental sociologists have examined why in some cases environmental impacts remain unnoticed, ignored, or tolerated, and in other cases are deemed unacceptable and demanding of immediate attention. In addition, they have identified how environmental impacts are distributed and experienced unequally, in many cases harming those who are already most vulnerable. While environmental impacts are very real in a biophysical sense, how they are perceived, framed, and understood by individuals, in the media, and throughout society determines which impacts are deemed problematic and if there will be a meaningful response.

Chapter 3 illustrates how the work of environmental sociologists has helped to identify the drivers of environmental impacts. While early and oversimplified explanations of environmental degradation focused on population growth alone, quantitative analysis has consistently revealed the important role of consumption and affluence in driving environmental impacts. Theoretical and empirical work also reveals how rising levels of consumption and affluence are being driven by a system that is growth-dependent, always producing more goods and services. This constant expansion results in increasing levels of pollution and depleted resource reserves. This chapter also describes how the concepts of the treadmill of production, the metabolic rift, and the second contradiction of capitalism contribute to our understanding of the underlying drivers of environmental degradation.

Chapter 4 focuses on possible solutions to environmental impacts, especially our escalating environmental crisis. This is the longest chapter in the book, because of the critical importance of identifying the most effective and just solutions. We will examine multiple perspectives on solution pathways. Reflexive modernization theory posits that society will respond to environmental harm through concern-driven counter-movements. Yet powerful economic and political groups continue to stymie such reflexivity. Ecological modernization theorists believe that through science, markets, and policy reform we can address environmental impacts and still support economic growth. In addition, widespread technological optimism promotes the notion that technology will be able to solve all of our environmental problems. In contrast, other scholars claim that in order to address our environmental crisis we must fundamentally change our social order. Some advocate for new priorities and policies, adopting alternative economic models, or creating a new system altogether.

Chapter 5 concludes the book by examining social movements and social transformation as well as possible areas for future work in environmental sociology. Social movements are critical for pushing forward solutions and system change. The environmental movement continues to grow, especially in response to climate change, and many groups are demanding structural social and economic changes. As these tensions increase, there will be more opportunities for environmental sociologists to understand and participate in these power struggles. In addition, as more environmental impacts inevitably unfold we need to examine the range of physical and emotional consequences, recognize and address injustices, and identify how communities can become stronger and more resilient in the face of change.

Environmental sociologists continue to do critical research that debunks false assumptions, seeks out effective and just solutions, and examines pathways for positive social transformation. Those who wish to pursue a career in environmental sociology stand poised to make important contributions to addressing our environmental challenges and identifying pathways to create a more just and sustainable world. Despite the existential threats we face and some already unavoidable impacts, there are still many possible paths forward and many ways we can do meaningful work to minimize global warming, species extinction, and human suffering. In other words, the path toward the most sustainable and just future is worth pursuing.

Discussion Questions

1. Why might it be problematic or even dangerous to separate "nature" and "society" in our academic disciplines and in our personal understanding of the world?
2. What is "the environment" and are we a part of it?
3. What is a theory? Why might theories be useful in the social sciences?
4. What makes "public sociology" different from other types of sociological research?

Suggested Reading

Bell, M. M., & L. L. Ashwood. (2015). Environmental problems and society. In *An Invitation to Environmental Sociology*. Fifth Edition. Los Angeles: Sage Publications.

Catton, W. R., & R. Dunlap. (1978). Environmental sociology: a new paradigm. *American Sociologist* 13: 41–49.

Dunlap, R. E. & W. R. Catton. (1979). Environmental sociology. *Annual Review of Sociology* 5: 243–273.

Gould, K. A., & T. L. Lewis. (2020). Theories in environmental sociology. In *Twenty Lessons in Environmental Sociology*. Edited by K. A. Gould and T. L. Lewis. New York: Oxford University Press.

Hannigan, J. (2014). Environmental sociology: key perspectives and controversies. In J. Hannigan, *Environmental Sociology*. Abingdon: Routledge.

Klinenberg, E., M. Araos & L. Koslov. (2020). Sociology and the climate crisis. *Annual Review of Sociology* 46: 649–669.

Lockie, S. (2015). What is environmental sociology? *Environmental Sociology* 1 (3): 139–142.

Aruffielle, M. D. & L. King. (2020). Introduction: Environmental problems require social solutions. In *Environmental Sociology: From Analysis to Action*. Edited by L. King and D. M. Auriffeille. Lanham, MD: Rowman & Littlefield.

York, R., & R. E. Dunlap. (2019). Environmental Sociology. In *The Wiley Blackwell Companion to Sociology*. Hoboken, NJ: John Wiley & Sons.

2
The Social Dimensions of Environmental Impacts

We begin by exploring environmental *impacts*, as environmental *problems* only emerge once people recognize certain impacts and decide that these impacts are undesirable or harmful. Yet, why is it that in some cases environmental impacts remain unnoticed, ignored, or tolerated, and in other cases they are deemed unacceptable and demanding of immediate attention? At what point does an impact become a risk, problem, or crisis? These questions reveal the important social dimensions of environmental impacts. It is not simply the case that scientists measure impacts and tell us there is a problem, their findings are widely accepted, and policies are implemented that effectively address the problem. Instead, social context, economics, power, and values shape science, how science is shared and perceived, how information is framed or suppressed, why some impacts seem riskier than others, and why impacts experienced by certain groups are more often overlooked or deemed unproblematic.

In this chapter, we will focus on how environmental sociologists study these important social dimensions of environmental impacts. This includes examining the role of science in assessing and understanding environmental impacts, and how science is conducted, shared, and interpreted. It also includes acknowledging that environmental risks, problems, and crises are *socially constructed* in that how they are socially perceived, framed, and understood matters, and ultimately shapes responses. Environmental sociologists have played an important role in exposing how environmental impacts are distributed and experienced unequally, with greater impacts experienced by minority and low-income communities.

The Role of Science: How Do We Know?

Environmental sociology is a social science that remains largely related to, and in many ways dependent upon, findings from the natural or biophysical sciences. Why do we care about plastic in the ocean? Because scientists have identified negative impacts of plastic pollution to ocean life and human health. The methods used by natural scientists represent our primary way of knowing and understanding the entities, processes, and relationships in the biophysical world. However, this is not to say that we should never question scientific findings, or that other ways of knowing have no value. While in most places the scientific method is the dominant way of knowing, it remains a social and imperfect process of trying to understand reality through the tools available.

Despite how it is often described, science is not a simple, unified, or predetermined process free of social influence. The science that helps us understand environmental impacts depends on what tools are used by scientists, what entities or processes are specifically measured, what methods are used to conduct these measurements, how the data is recorded and analyzed, and how findings are interpreted and communicated. In addition, funding sources and vested interests can influence how science is conducted, shared, or, in some cases, suppressed. In other words, science can tell us different things depending on how the science is conducted, interpreted, and communicated. Set scientific practices and standards aim to minimize possible variation in results, yet science is still a social practice and therefore some degree of skepticism is always warranted. Despite its social nature and the possibilities of flaws and imperfections, science remains our primary way of understanding the biophysical world and continues to play a key role in identifying and understanding environmental impacts.

Environmental impacts are very real; however, how we think and talk about them matters. This relates to debates about realism versus social constructionism. While an extreme social constructionist position would argue that our understanding of the world is based solely on our individual perceptions and thoughts, this view is not widely supported. For example, if someone were to argue that this book only exists because you think it is a book, most people would agree that the book physically exists apart from what you think of it. Scholars have convincingly argued that the extreme constructionist position fails to acknowledge the importance of the nonhuman entities and processes in our world and can be dangerous if used to undermine the rationale for environmental protection. For example, if all of nature is socially constructed, then only our thoughts about it matter. Most environmental sociologists are realists and believe that a real, material world exists independent of human thoughts and perceptions. Yet they also largely agree that constructionist insights are critical to understanding the social dimensions of impacts that ultimately shape responses. We base our work on the reality of a biophysical world, independent of human thoughts and ideas, but accept that human knowledge about this world is inherently socially constructed and that our perceptions, ideas, and practices continue to shape environmental relationships and outcomes.

Environmental sociologists have proposed different theoretical approaches to guide research that acknowledges the dual importance of realism and social constructionism. For example, Freudenburg and others (1995: 387) explain the idea of *conjoint constitution*. They argue that the social and the biophysical worlds are "conjointly constituted" and connected like "opposing poles of a magnet." Vickery and others (2020) apply this concept to understand the relationships between forest change due to bark beetle outbreaks, perceptions of these changes, and how these perceptions influence support for certain forest management practices. Another example is Carolan's (2005) use of critical realism to develop a stratified conception of nature, emphasizing how the biophysical and social aspects of the world overlap and shape each other. Houser and colleagues (2017) apply Carolan's framework to understand how farmers perceive the biophysical changes they are experiencing due to climate change, and in turn how these perceptions shape their beliefs concerning climate change and participation in mitigation actions. These approaches, among others, provide guidance for environmental sociologists to navigate the dual importance of the biophysical and social dimensions of environmental impacts.

While science is critical for understanding biophysical changes, it can only tell us so much about environmental impacts. If we know how many parts per million of a chemical is in our air or water and we know that this amount is higher than it was a year ago, is it harmful? At what concentration does it become problematic? If animal tests show that there is a cancer-causing chemical in a cosmetic, does that mean it will cause cancer in humans? Should it be banned? Who decides if a certain concentration or dose is acceptable or not? Standards set by government, such as the US Environmental Protection Agency or the Food and Drug Administration, are "based on science." However, the determination of the acceptable levels of chemical contamination remains a social process influenced by power, economics, and values.

Science is often contested, not only because it is an imperfect process with inherent uncertainties, but because the implications of scientific findings often have social and economic consequences. Environmental sociologists have studied the role of scientists and experts in assessing environmental impacts, the standards and assumptions used in science, the priorities and values that are privileged in science and the media, and whose voices are heard and whose are ignored. Science is often contested to protect vested interests. Thus, in many cases, environmental issues will not be solved simply through more science, but through confronting political and economic power. One clear example is how climate science has been deliberately disputed, attacked, and undermined by fossil fuel companies and other powerful groups.

Climate science has been contested not because the evidence is unclear, but because of what this evidence implies in terms of causes and solutions. The fossil fuel industry, conservative think tanks, and other vested interests have worked to undermine climate science and perpetuate climate denialism. The conservative movement worked to undermine climate science by creating scientific controversy and a "debate" about climate change, which deterred climate policy and created politically polarized views on the climate crisis (e.g., McCright and Dunlap 2010, Dunlap and McCright 2011, 2015). In a coordinated campaign over the past several decades, vested interests (e.g., vested in fossil fuels, transportation, or other carbon-intensive industries) designed public relations schemes to emphasize the uncertainties of climate science, promote pseudo-science, and personally attack leading climate scientists (Brulle 2014, Brulle and Roberts 2017). Thus, the "debate" over climate science, and therefore climate denialism, was strategically manufactured to delay and impede climate policy. As put by Brulle (2018a: 256), "at its core, this is a bad faith debate and only serves as a proxy argument to protect vested corporate interests." In Chapter 4, we will discuss how these vested interests not only shaped how climate impacts have been perceived, but continue to delay and undermine possible solutions.

Public Sociology: Exposing Efforts to Undermine Climate Science

Environmental sociologists' work examining the climate science "debate" and the overall attack on climate science represents an important example of public sociology. McCright and Dunlap's work uncovering the climate denial "machine" was discussed in a wide range of media outlets including *The Washington Post*, *The Guardian*, and *The New York Times*. Robert Brulle and Timmons Roberts (2017) explain how in 2016, a US senator stood on the Senate floor and, referring to Riley Dunlap, Aaron McCright, Justin Farrell, and others, stated:

> The scholarship of all these academics, all these organiz-ations, and all these authors—the detectives who are

exposing the Web of Denial—have shined a bright light into its dark corners and illuminated its concerted effort to dupe the American public and sabotage climate action in America, all to protect the fossil fuel industry that funds it.

In addition, Timmons Roberts met regularly with senators about misinformation efforts and Robert Brulle (2014, 2018a, 2018b) exposed funding sources and networks of organizations involved in climate science misinformation and denial campaigns. Brulle's work was discussed in *The Guardian* and *The New York Times,* and he published a 2016 piece in *The Washington Post* titled, "America has been duped on climate change." While denial and misinformation campaigns have been effective at stymying climate action, public opinion polls indicate that a growing majority now believe we must address the climate crisis. The work of environmental sociologists has and continues to be publicly valuable, exposing efforts to undermine climate science and helping to counter misinformation campaigns.

Understanding environmental impacts can also focus on nonhuman species, illustrating how we can move away from an anthropocentric view of impacts. Science tells us that extinction rates are rising and population numbers for many species are in decline. However, more research is needed to provide a sociological understanding of biodiversity loss (Besek and York 2019). Research and scholarship grounded in the subfield of critical animal studies continue to reveal how we can focus on nonhumans in our understanding of relationships, ethics, and community. Human and nonhuman animal histories are interwoven, and the climate and ecological crises will adversely affect all species (Stuart and Gunderson 2020). In addition, new materialist or neo-materialist approaches in sociology continue to increase attention toward nonhuman entities and actors and the relationships between the biophysical and the social, reinforcing how nature and society are far from separate realms. Moving further away from an anthropocentric focus, research and scholarship in environmental sociology is increasingly extending to include an examination of nonhuman beings and entities. Science continues to be critical for understanding these relationships and reimagining configurations with more positive outcomes.

While science is a social and imperfect process, it remains critical for identifying and understanding environmental impacts. Environmental sociologists continue to incorporate the work of natural scientists in their research and are also increasingly collaborating on interdisciplinary studies to understand social and ecological impacts together. Beyond being understood as an *impact*, environmental changes can also be understood as *risks*, *problems*, or *crises*. Yet the social construction of environmental impacts as risks, problems, and crises involves much more than simply gathering and presenting the scientific evidence.

Environmental Impacts as Risks and Problems

While a study can reveal the extent of pollution, how many degrees the average global temperature has increased, or how many Bengal tigers are left in the world, these scientific findings can be interpreted and understood in a wide range of ways. It matters how scientific information is conducted and shared, but also how it is perceived, framed, and understood by individuals, in the media, and throughout society. Scientific findings are communicated and interpreted socially in the context of economics, power, values, and ethics. For example, a large oil spill might be interpreted as negative or problematic depending on: the economic impact on the fishing industry, the visible aesthetic and ecological impacts, or the loss of animal and plant life. But at what point is the spill publicly considered a "disaster" or a "crisis"?

There can be a wide range of different interpretations, framings, and responses to scientific information about environmental impacts. Therefore, constructionist scholarship on environmental issues remains critical. Again, it must be emphasized that when environmental sociologists examine how environmental risks and problems are "socially constructed," this does not mean that these impacts are not biophysically real, only that how they are understood, framed, and responded to is a social process with important implications. Environmental changes and impacts are detected all the time, but in what cases are they considered a risk and when does a risk turn into a problem?

Risk is an important concept in environmental sociology. Risk is a social construct because people define risk differently, even when their assessment is based on the same information. Risk perception is often based more on emotional responses and social context than on science or actual probability. For example, the chances of a shark attack or an airplane crash are very low compared to a car crash, yet air travel and swimming in the ocean are largely considered to be higher risk than driving. Activities that we have control over typically seem less risky. In addition, impacts that occur in the future or that develop slowly over time are largely considered less risky than impacts that happen immediately and can be easily observed. Science can be used in risk calculation, yet how risks are calculated remains a social process as well.

Ulrich Beck's seminal work, *Risk Society* (1992), describes how we have come into an age of manufactured risks as a result of technological innovations, economic growth, and industrialization. As humans have created new technologies and production processes in the name of "progress," risks are created and, like a boomerang, come back to negatively impact us. Examples include the use of agricultural chemicals, nuclear power, and plastics. Jens Zinn (2016) explains that because of the significant extent that humans have reshaped nature, we are moving from a period of risk avoidance and minimization into a phase where we must accept more risks and focus on risk-taking and risk management. In other words, environmental risks have become increasingly unavoidable and, therefore, we must now focus on which risks to take and how to mitigate these risks. As human activities have resulted in unavoidable impacts such as microplastic pollution and global climate change, more risk has become the norm.

One area where risk remains critical is in understanding the impacts of toxic chemicals found in everyday products like shampoo, cosmetics, cleaning supplies, food packaging, and electronics. While many chemicals are banned in Europe, very few are banned in the US. These chemicals may cause birth defects, hormone disruption, neurological damage, cancer, and reproductive disorders. Due to the inherent limitations in studying human exposure to toxins, including the inability to do controlled tests on humans and the sheer number of different contaminates that can interact in the environment, in many cases human impacts are uncertain. Yet even when tests on animals indicate that a substance is a hazard, the risks to humans are often disputed, with different interpretations of findings and the possible impacts. Environmental sociologists have examined the intersection of science and risk in terms of the regulation of toxins, revealing how expert science and definitions of risk can be contested to protect vested interests and how a focus only on scientific data is shortsighted when economics, power, and politics shape perceptions, framing, and policy responses (e.g., Brown 2007, Cordner 2016).

When risk is contested, what determines how risk is used to shape policy and regulations? In *Toxic Safety*, Alissa Cordner (2016) examines how different interest groups interpret science and define risk differently and why these differences are important. Over four years, Cordner conducted 116 in-depth interviews with different stakeholders involved in debates over the science, risk, and regulation of flame retardants. Flame retardants can be found in many household items (e.g., furniture and electronics) and are associated with endocrine disruption, cancer, and neurological and reproductive problems. Cordner's work reveals how different interest groups, such as the chemical industry, interpret science differently, and also create alternative definitions of (and formulas to calculate) risk. The book illustrates how "strategic science translation" as well "strategic risk definition" are used to support different positions on the use of flame retardants. In the face of inherent scientific uncertainties and powerful vested interests, science and risk are constructed differently to support specific goals. While regulation is supposed to be based on science and a scientific risk assessment, a scientist at the Environmental Protection Agency (EPA) told Cordner that ultimately "deciding what to do is not a science question." It is more a matter of the power of stakeholders and the social, political, and economic forces at play. Unfortunately, when industrial actors work to prevent and delay regulation, this occurs at the expense of public health and safety.

Public Sociology: Working with Communities, NGOs, and Regulators on Toxins

Alissa Cordner, Lauren Richter, and Paul Brown published an article in 2019 highlighting different avenues in which their work studying highly fluorinated compounds has contributed to public sociology. Highly fluorinated compounds are found in Teflon, Scotchguard, and semiconductor devices, among many other uses. These chemicals are extremely persistent in the environment and in the human body and are known to cause birth defects, cancer, and disruptions to the thyroid and immune system. Their work involved a wide range of stakeholders from the start, including impacted communities and regulatory agencies. They explain,

> Our proposed model of engaged public sociology sees the researcher as a reflexive and observant participant in the environmental and social justice movements they study or the environmental topics they investigate. This approach deliberately focuses knowledge production on issues and inequalities of concern to impacted and marginalized communities. (Cordner et al. 2019: 341)

They worked with environmental groups including the Environmental Working Group (EWG), participated in government assessments and regulatory processes, served on advisory committees, and advised government agencies on how to investigate highly fluorinated compounds. They also worked with the EWG to create an interactive map displaying contamination information, which was featured in *USA Today*, *Time*, and the *Huffington Post*. Community members were able to use this interactive map to discover contamination sites in their neighborhoods. While there were many challenges involved, including finding stakeholders' common interests and making tradeoffs between time and effort invested and the ability to publish peer-reviewed work, Cordner and others (2019: 348) felt that the "drawbacks are absolutely worth the potential benefits of engaged scholarship and advocacy."

Climate impacts represent another example of the importance of understanding risk perception. While scientists tell us climate change poses a significant risk, there are a range of different perceptions about the risks of climate change. Climate change is an environmental phenomenon that is perceived as a threat differentially, depending on both social and biophysical factors. Climate change risk perception is influenced by biophysical changes and events and how those changes are experienced and interpreted, by media framing, and by social context and identity (Olofsson et al. 2016). Special interests, values, and market logic also shape how climate change is framed as a risk (Zinn 2016). In addition, human psychology, culture, and emotions influence our perceptions of climate change. In *Living in Denial* (2011), Kari Norgaard illustrates how identity, culture, and human psychology can result in widespread "socially organized denial" about the extent of risks posed by climate change. When something is as massive and threatening as climate change, it is understandable that many people would rather not think about it.

Climate change also continues to occur slowly and is not obvious on a daily basis. Because climate change can be difficult to perceive, some people might not be particularly concerned, especially if immediate needs are not being met. However, extreme climate-related events are increasing attention and concern. Environmental sociologists continue to examine perceptions of climate change as a risk through both quantitative and qualitative analyses. For example, in a quantitative cross-national public opinion study, Kyle Knight (2016) found that climate change risk perception was higher in countries that were wealthier, left-leaning, and also more vulnerable. In a qualitative study, Kevin Gotham (2016) used field observations, document analysis, and personal interviews to understand the construction of climate risk and conflicts over risk-reduction activities in coastal communities of Southern Louisiana. As climate change continues to have significant environmental impacts—including hurricanes, floods, droughts, and heat waves—individuals will be increasingly experiencing disasters and noticeable changes in their physical environment that will likely increase climate change risk perception (McKinzie 2019).

If an environmental impact is effectively communicated and widely perceived as a risk, at what point is this impact considered an environmental problem? John Hannigan (2014) describes a detailed process for the construction of environmental problems involving scientists, politicians, journalists, and activists. Key tasks in constructing an environmental problem include: 1) assembling, 2) presenting, and 3) contesting. Different actors participate in different tasks. *Assembling* involves the activities of science to discover and measure an impact or condition and naming the problem. *Presenting* relates to media coverage and attention, visibility, and communicating the moral implications of impacts. *Contesting* includes the mobilization around an issue, political and legal battles, and policy debates. Hannigan explains that certain factors are generally necessary for successful construction; these include: scientific authority, bringing the science into the environmental movement, media attention and framing, visual and symbolic dramatization, economic incentives, and institutional sponsors to legitimate the problem and push for the issue to be addressed.

Climate change is increasingly considered a problem, with higher and higher levels of public concern. For example, a 2019 US public opinion poll found that more than a quarter of Americans consider climate change a "crisis," with an additional 36 percent defining it as a "serious problem" (CBS News 2019). In addition, 60 percent of Americans polled think government should do something to address global warming and 70 percent believe environmental protection is more important than economic growth (Marlon et al. 2020). In the United Kingdom (UK), 85 percent of citizens are concerned about climate change, 52 percent are very concerned, and 55 percent think the UK should bring emissions to net zero before 2050 targets (Dickman and Skinner 2019).

Environmental sociologists have used public opinion polls to assess how overall views and perceptions of climate change have changed over time, as well as what factors influence individuals' views the most. For example, research has shown that actual climatic changes and events have very little impact on climate change perceptions, which are more influenced by political orientation (Marquart-Pyatt et al. 2014). Other researchers compared the influence of extreme weather events, access to scientific information, elite cues, media coverage, and economic factors, and found that the opinions expressed by elite political actors remained the most influential factor (Carmichael and Brulle 2017). These findings, among others, illustrate how politics and power continue to shape the public perception of environmental problems.

Media coverage also remains critical in shaping public perceptions of environmental impacts. This involves not only the extent of coverage but also how an issue is being framed in the media. Framing is important in how environmental and social problems are defined and understood. For example, Norah MacKendrick (2010) examined the framing of chemical body burdens (how much contamination exists in the body) as a social problem in the Canadian news media between 1986 to 2006. Framing shifted over these years to emphasize body burdens and chemical contamination as an individual problem and a risk to be managed by individuals through consumption choices (more on this in Chapter 4). The framing of environmental impacts in the media continues to be highly influential, not only in shaping how a problem is identified and understood, but also how causes are diagnosed and how specific solutions are justified.

Media framing is especially important in understanding public perceptions of climate change. Climate media coverage aided efforts to deny and counter climate science through a journalistic focus on a balanced presentation of competing views, giving excessive attention to a small minority of denialists (McCright and Dunlap 2015). This "false balance" narrative was most prevalent in the US, whereas in many other countries media narratives widely accepted the reality of climate change and instead focused on possible solutions (Stoddart et al. 2017). In addition, different media sources frame climate change in different ways, and individuals often seek out sources that support their personal positions and biases, creating what some call "reinforcing spirals" or "echo chambers" (Bolin and Hamilton 2018). However, as public opinions about climate change have shifted and climate change is increasingly framed as a problem of high concern in the media, it is more commonly referred to as the *climate crisis*.

Environmental Impacts as Crises

In addition to being considered a *problem*, environmental impacts can be considered a *crisis*. General definitions of a crisis include: a condition of precarity or danger, a crucial time or decisive moment, a critical period that determines all future events, threats to primary goals, extreme trouble, being affected by serious problems, and a time of great difficulty. In addition, a crisis can be a situation when the current system can no longer be maintained and a transformation is necessary. Evidence suggests that, in terms of all of these different meanings, we are facing multiple crises that together create a state of environmental crisis.

The crisis most discussed is the climate crisis. In 2019, several major media outlets specifically chose to abandon the term "climate change" and to instead use the terms "climate crisis," "climate emergency," or "climate breakdown." These terms are also increasingly used by scientists, journalists, and academics. As explained by Eric Klinenberg and others (2020: 650) in the *Annual Review of Sociology*, "we use the term climate crisis rather than climate change to reflect a terminology that more accurately captures the condition of urgency and danger engendered by a heated world." As stated above, a 2019 US public opinion poll revealed that more than a quarter of Americans considered climate change a "crisis" (CBS News 2019). The word "emergency" is also used increasingly to describe global warming. A 2019 article representing the views of 11,000 scientists published in *BioScience* was titled "World Scientists' Warning of a Climate Emergency" (Ripple et al. 2019). As scientists, media outlets, and others increasingly frame climate change as a *crisis* or *emergency*, more sociological research is needed to examine these framings and how they influence public opinion and public support for climate action.

The terms "ecological crisis" and "biodiversity crisis" are also now commonly used by scientists and in the media. While many people overlook human dependency on other species, scientists continue to argue that at the current rates of extinction we will alter the natural world in ways that threaten not only human well-being but also human existence (Ceballos et al. 2015). The concept of ecosystem services has been used for decades to emphasize the ways that humans benefit from and depend on ecosystems (Reid et al. 2005) and projections of global change reveal the potential severity of social impacts from biodiversity loss. The IPBES media release (2019) states that species loss has accelerated to rates that could cross ecological thresholds, resulting in a cascade of extinctions and threats to human existence. Because many people fail to see the connections between human society and other species, the threat of biodiversity loss is largely overlooked. Further sociological attention is needed to understand biodiversity loss in general (see Besek and York 2019), including the construction of biodiversity loss as a social problem and how the framing of biodiversity loss as the "biodiversity crisis" or an "ecological emergency" shapes public concern.

Environmental impacts need not be existential or at a global scale to be considered a crisis, as clearly illustrated by the water crisis in Flint, Michigan that began in 2014. The Flint water crisis represents one of the most devastating regional environmental impacts in recent decades. Flint residents were exposed to water contaminated with harmful levels of lead for two years, while local government officials reassured them that the water was safe to drink (Fasenfest

2019). The case of Flint illustrates the importance of vocalizing concerns, gathering scientific evidence, and mobilizing key players and activist groups to create public recognition of a crisis.

The concerns of Flint residents about their water eventually resulted in the acknowledgment of a crisis, but after significant delay and serious impacts (see Krings et al. 2019). When the water source was switched by emergency management to save money, residents started to notice that the water tasted bad, was discolored, and smelled off. Residents protested, displaying bottles of discolored water. Local officials argued that the complaints were exaggerated and dismissed concerns. Even after General Motors noticed the change in water quality at their manufacturing plant and negotiated a way to switch sources, the concerns of residents continued to be ignored. One resident reached out to scientists to test their water and they discovered harmful levels of lead. This initiated a growing collaborative effort between activist groups, residents, and scientists to illustrate the extent of lead contamination. This contamination, however, was still not considered a crisis and was ignored by national media outlets for months. Only after the state government was pressured to switch the water supply back to the previous source did national news outlets call it a crisis, focusing on the health impacts to residents—especially to young children. This crisis resulted in permanent damage to the Flint water system, severe public health impacts, and criminal charges. As explained by Paul Mohai (2018), the Flint water crisis represents one of the most "egregious" examples of environmental injustice in US history.

The Unequal Distribution of Impacts

When examining environmental impacts, it is critical to identify *who* is affected by these impacts. Environmental injustice or inequality refers to a reoccurring pattern in the distribution of environmental impacts: people who have less power due to race or economic status experience the harms of environmental impacts disproportionately. While race, gender, and class are socially constructed and symbolic categories, they continue to have real-world, significant consequences. It is an injustice when certain people face more impacts than others. When environmental impacts are overlooked, accepted, or justified based on race it is called *environmental racism* (Bullard 1993, Pellow 2005, Taylor 2014). Environmental injustice can be intentional or unintentional, and in either case, the goal of the environmental justice movement is to identify and address cases of injustice.

Environmental justice is a global social movement, a concept that is increasingly influencing policy and the policy process, and a growing area of research. The UK-based Environmental Justice Foundation (2020) works globally to ensure that "environmental security is a basic human right." Greenpeace (2020) states that environmental justice "guarantees that all people have equal access to a healthy, safe, and sustainable environment, as well as equal protection from environmental harm." The US Environmental Protection Agency (2020) defines environmental justice as "ensuring the same degree of protection from environmental and health hazards" and providing "equal access to the decision-making process to have a healthy environment in which to live, learn, and work." Research in environmental justice has evolved over the past few decades to examine not only toxic exposures but also transportation, housing, energy, and local and global issues, as well as the intersectionality of race, gender, class, disablement, age, and other characteristics (Malin and Ryder 2018).

Environmental justice involves an equal right to safe living for all: no one should be considered expendable. People who are already vulnerable or marginalized face increased and intersecting health risks. For example, low-income people of color face disproportionately high rates of asthma from poor air quality, a condition that makes them more vulnerable to other health risks, including the Covid-19 virus. Such trends represent an ongoing form of violence perpetuated by systemic racism. As explained by Stewart Lockie (2018: 177–78), environmental injustices "shorten peoples' lives, compromise their physical and mental health, and increase their vulnerability to other sources of risk" and such injustice is a form of "violence perpetuated on the bodies, minds and livelihoods of its victims." Fighting for environmental justice, therefore, involves demanding that environmental and public health laws and regulations provide all people *equal and adequate* protection from these forms of violence (Mohai et al. 2009).

In the US, environmental justice research initially focused on how African-American communities have experienced a greater burden of environmental health impacts. In 1982, activists organized to stop the state of North Carolina from dumping 120 million pounds of soil contaminated with polychlorinated biphenyls (PCBs) in Warren County, the county with the highest proportion of African-American residents. This brought the issue of environmental racism to national attention and triggered an increased focus on similar cases nationwide. These cases continue to be identified, including the Flint water crisis, where racism and lack of political power resulted in the health concerns of residents being repeatedly ignored, minimized, and dismissed (Mohai 2018). In general, minority, low-income, and immigrant communities continue to face more environmental harm and associated health impacts. Health impacts from exposure to chemicals, pollution, and toxins include cancer, birth defects, asthma, nervous system disorders, hormone disruption, and other acute and chronic illnesses.

Over time, environmental justice has expanded beyond a focus on the unequal distribution of environmental harms. Other forms of injustice examined include: lack of access to environmental benefits or resources, unequal participation in environmental decision-making, lack of recognition of community needs or interests, and degrading land uses on sites of cultural importance (Schlosberg 2013). Studies also expanded to focus on a diversity of different groups, including Latino immigrants, Native Americans, and other indigenous people. In addition, environmental justice research and activism has spread internationally and taken on a global focus, including increasing attention to climate justice (Schlosberg and Collins 2014).

Environmental sociologists continue to make important contributions in identifying cases of environmental injustice and, in almost all cases, this work represents examples of public sociology. For example, research that identifies impacts on vulnerable communities alone is socially beneficial, as it is essential information to raise awareness of an issue and support efforts to protect communities. Many environmental sociologists also take their work beyond identifying impacts and also study and participate in social movements fighting for environmental justice and/or work with policymakers to incorporate environmental justice into laws and regulations. Much of this research has been done in collaboration with vulnerable communities, was designed to serve these communities, and has resulted in policy and planning outcomes that help protect communities. While there are many important studies in this area of research, here we look at selected work to highlight key themes and findings.

Extensive research has focused on unequal impacts to African-American communities in both urban and rural settings. In *Dumping in Dixie* (1990, 2008), Robert Bullard identified how institutional racism and a lack of political and economic power resulted in a disproportionate number of toxic waste facilities and environmental hazards being located in African-American communities in the US South. In *Garbage Wars* (2002), David Pellow describes historical conflicts over solid waste disposal sites in Chicago, with waste incinerators disproportionately being placed in African-American neighborhoods. One explanation of this trend is decision-making along the "path of least resistance": locating undesirable facilities in places where residents have less education, income, political power, and time to participate in collective opposition. For years, it was debated whether hazardous facilities were being placed in low-income and minority communities or if low-income and minority people were moving into areas with these facilities—known as a "chicken or the egg" question. Dorceta Taylor's book *Toxic Communities* (2014) explains how this question is complicated and influenced by discriminatory zoning laws, land prices, segregation, gentrification, and the manipulative tactics of profit-hungry corporations. Environmental sociologists continue to use qualitative methods as well as quantitative and spatial analysis to identify cases of environmental injustice.

Environmental sociologists have also examined how Native Americans have faced and continue to face high burdens of environmental pollution and hazards. This is especially evident in cases of uranium mining and hazardous waste disposal on Native American lands. In other cases, tribes face environmental changes that degrade their culture and traditional practices. For example, the culture and values of Native Americans were dismissed in Northern Arizona when permission was granted for a ski resort to create artificial snow from reclaimed sewage water on a sacred Navajo and Hopi site (Schlosberg and Carruthers 2010). Research has also illustrated how environmental decline impacts diet, health, and emotional responses within the Karuk Tribe of Northern California (Norgaard et al. 2011, 2017, Norgaard and Reed 2017). Increasingly research is also focusing on the loss of "first foods," the ability to practice spirituality, and increasing climate vulnerability in Native American populations (Vickery and Hunter 2014).

Other work has exposed environmental racism in Latino communities in the US. For example, in their book *The Slums of Aspen* (2011), Lisa Sun-Hee Park and David Pellow reveal environmental privilege and injustice found in the elite resort town Aspen, Colorado—where minority immigrant workers serve wealthy visitors and residents. They discuss how even mainstream environmental groups illustrate nativist environmentalism, a type of racism linked to entitlement, and support anti-immigrant positions. In addition, research on pesticide drift illustrates a clear lack of protections for California migrant farmworkers and agricultural communities, how communities are fighting for protection, and the increasing political conflicts over agricultural pesticides (Harrison 2011, 2014).

With existential environmental crises accelerating, we also see a globally focused environmental justice movement. Globally, colonization, unequal exchange, and power relations have benefitted wealthy countries and degraded poor countries (Givens et al. 2019). For example, countries from the Global North continue to extract resources from poor countries. In addition, they are now outsourcing polluting industries to countries in the Global South and also directly shipping toxic waste to these countries. Local communities and nongovernmental organizations (NGOs) attempt to resist these injustices and continue to fight against the global toxics trade (Pellow 2007, 2011). The unequal global distribution of environmental harms and unequal global exchange, through resource extraction and waste deposition, has contributed to a range of environmental problems including climate change, biodiversity loss, and pollution.

Climate justice at both a local and a global scale has become an increasingly important topic in environmental sociology. At a local scale, events like Hurricane Katrina illustrate how low-income and minority communities are more vulnerable to climate impacts, living in more vulnerable areas with fewer means to avoid harm (Schlosberg and Collins 2014). In climate politics, especially in discussions of a Green New Deal, more attention is being focused on how to best protect vulnerable front-line communities who will face the most severe impacts from hurricanes, floods, drought, heat, and disease. Already we have seen how the impacts of hurricanes Katrina and Harvey disproportionately affected African-Americans. Robert Bullard continues to work with communities, NGOs, and policymakers to protect front-line communities, arguing that our climate strategies need an explicit focus on justice, as all communities do not experience climate change equally. In addition, more attention is being given to global scale climate justice and how people in the Global South, who have contributed very little to overall carbon emissions, now face the most severe impacts with the least amount of resources for adaptation and survival (Roberts and Parks 2006, Harlan et al. 2015). Climate change will continue to affect marginalized communities most severely, and research and activism are both needed to reveal vulnerabilities and protect communities.

Public Sociology: Native American Climate Vulnerabilities

Native Americans have strong physical, spiritual, and cultural connections to their territorial landscapes, and indigenous diets, health, knowledge, and livelihoods are increasingly threatened by climate change. Native Americans have already faced many conditions that have increased their overall burden of physical and mental health risks. Climate change, and the associated changes in Native environments, only adds to these risks by further impacting food sources, ecosystems, physical health, and mental well-being. In addition to the research on the Karuk Tribe that Kari Norgaard conducted with Ron Reed on health, diet, gender practices, and mental health, Norgaard also wrote and co-authored important policy-relevant reports assessing the vulnerability of the Karuk Tribe and climate change adaptation options. In a 2014 report, titled "Karuk Traditional Ecological Knowledge and the Need for Knowledge Sovereignty," Norgaard details how the criminalization of traditional Karuk management activities and denial of access to subsistence and customary activities impairs the continuation and generation of critical indigenous knowledge. This results in negative impacts on diet and physical health, and psychological stress. In a 2016 report titled "Karuk Tribe Climate Vulnerability Assessment," Norgaard (with noted contributions from others) identifies the climate impacts in the region, especially changes in the traditional fire regime, and the range of impacts on the Karuk Tribe. As Norgaard (2016: 6) explains,

> Impacts to culturally significant species in the face of climate change have thus more direct impacts on Karuk people than for communities who no longer retain such intimate connections with other beings and places in the natural world. Yet part of the increased vulnerabilities Karuk people face as the climate changes are a direct result of the strength of these connections.

In 2019, along with William Tripp, Kari Norgaard co-authored the "Karuk Climate Adaptation Plan" which elaborates on climate impacts and also details adaptation options that can be considered to address acute emergencies, long-term restoration, and ecosystem resilience, as well as to help alleviate impacts including impairment of diet, physical health, and mental health. This work is important to identify vulnerabilities, coordinate with organizations and agencies, and make plans to best protect the Karuk Tribe as climate change impacts intensify. Indigenous communities in general, with close physical and cultural ties to land, will be heavily impacted by the biophysical changes of global warming and will need to adapt to preserve livelihoods, health, and culture.

There is an important moral imperative to identify and address cases of environmental injustice. Populations that are most vulnerable and have already faced disproportionate risks and inadequate resources continue to bear the majority of the burden of environmental impacts. Even when one is in a privileged position, with the ability to overlook or turn away from these injustices, doing so only makes one morally complicit in the outcomes. Identifying and exposing cases of environmental injustice continues to be a critical way that environmental sociologists can help to protect marginalized and vulnerable communities.

The Social Dimensions Matter

Identifying, assessing, and communicating environmental impacts is far from being a simple, straightforward process. Some people continue to describe the "science-policy interface" as a linear progression of research, information, policy, and action. Yet, the actual relationships are vastly different from this idealized, oversimplified narrative. They are strongly influenced by other social dimensions, including power, economics, and values. In many cases, these social dimensions are even more important than the scientific evidence in determining whether impacts are considered risks, problems, or crises and if they will be addressed or ignored.

Science remains the primary way to measure impacts, but science can only tell us so much. For example, science can tell us that there are over 415 parts per million of carbon dioxide in the atmosphere, but at what exact concentration did or does this become a problem? When is this considered a crisis? By whom and why? These are all critical questions related to the social dimensions, rather than the biophysical dimensions, of climate change. In addition, biophysical science remains an activity inherently influenced by social processes and can be communicated and framed in different ways. While environmental sociologists are generally realists, who believe in a biophysical world apart from social perspectives, it is clear that understanding the social dimensions of impacts remains extremely important.

In addition, we have seen that it matters *who* environmental impacts affect. In a society with institutionalized racism and injustices, those who are already marginalized and are the most vulnerable continue to face a disproportionate burden of environmental impacts. As minority and low-income communities tend to have less power and political influence, they continue to bear the brunt of impacts in terms of impaired livelihoods and physical and mental health. Environmental sociologists continue to play a key role in identifying, politicizing, and addressing cases of environmental injustice.

Discussion Questions

1. What is the role of natural science in environmental sociology?
2. What is the difference between a social constructionist and a realist perspective?
3. What are some environmental impacts you view as high risk or low risk? Why?
4. What makes an environmental impact a problem or a crisis?
5. What are environmental justice activists, scholars, and organizations fighting for?
6. What are some examples of climate justice at different geographic scales?

Suggested Reading

Angelo, H., & C. Jerolmack. (2020). Nature's Looking Glass. In *Environmental Sociology: From Analysis to Action.* Edited by L. King & D. M. Auriffeille. Lanham, MD: Rowman & Littlefield.

Brulle, R. J., & J. T. Roberts. (2017). Climate misinformation campaigns and public sociology. *Contexts* 16(1): 78–79.

Cordner, A., L. Richter, & P. Brown. (2019). Environmental chemicals and public sociology: engaged scholarship on highly fluorinated compounds. *Environmental Sociology* 5(4): 339–351.

Givens, J. E., X. Huang, & A. K. Jorgenson. (2019). Ecologically unequal exchange: A theory of global environmental injustice. *Sociology Compass* 13(5): e12693.

Hannigan, J. (2014). Chapters 3–7. *Environmental Sociology.* London: Routledge.

MacKendrick, N. (2020). The sociology of environmental health. In *Twenty Lessons in Environmental Sociology.* Edited by K. A. Gould & T. L. Lewis. New York: Oxford University Press.

McCright, A., & R. Dunlap. (2015). Challenging climate change: The denial countermovement. In *Climate Change and Society: Sociological Perspectives.* Edited by R. E. Dunlap & R. J. Brulle. New York: Oxford University Press.

Mohai, P., D. Pellow, & J. T. Roberts. (2009). Environmental justice. *Annual Review of Environment and Resources* 34: 405–430.

Norgaard, K. (2020). Normalizing the unthinkable: Climate denial and everyday life. In *Twenty Lessons in Environmental Sociology.* Edited by K. A. Gould & T. L. Lewis. New York: Oxford University Press.

Pellow, D. (2017). *What Is Critical Environmental Justice?* Cambridge: Polity.

3
Examining Drivers of Environmental Impacts

In order to address environmental impacts, we must first identify the drivers and root causes of these impacts. Treating the symptoms will only get us so far, as such approaches leave the source of environmental harm intact. We must understand what specific human actions are resulting in negative environmental impacts and, more importantly, what aspects of our social system allow, influence, or encourage these actions. While some people may believe that environmental impacts are simply the result of human population growth, quantitative studies have debunked this oversimplified explanation. Instead, other factors, including consumption, urbanization, and economic growth, have been identified as important determinants of environmental impacts globally. Studies have also identified characteristics at the individual and household levels that are associated with greater environmental impacts. Quantitative studies at multiple scales continue to play an important role in identifying the drivers of impacts.

Social theory also plays an important role in understanding the drivers of environmental impacts. Certain theories posit that the drivers of impacts are systemic. This means that the drivers are related to the way we have organized our society, or our social structure. In other words, impacts are largely a result of the priorities and goals that structure and give order to our society and our cumulative actions. While many people believe that society is organized in a way that is normal, natural, or common-sense, this is likely (and understandably) because it is what they have known. The current social order is actually relatively recent, and unique in human history. Social theory continues to inform debates about what specifically in our system is driving us further into environmental crisis. Is it simply a matter of technological innovation, economic development, and policy reform, or is the way our system is designed inherently problematic and driving us toward ecological and social collapse? These debates about the drivers of impacts have important implications in terms of what solutions should be considered.

In addition to systemic or structural drivers, our social order also reinforces and is shaped by beliefs and ways of thinking which can drive environmental impacts. As we explored in Chapter 2, social ideas and perceptions matter because they shape how we view environmental impacts. In addition, ideas and perceptions shape how we interact with the biophysical world. In many cases, ideologies—what we believe exists, is good or bad, and what is possible (Therborn 1980)—influence how we view and interpret the world as well as how we individually and collectively act, including actions that cause environmental harm. In addition, certain ideologies conceal the underlying structural drivers of environmental impacts.

In this chapter, we will explore how environmental sociologists work to identify global influences, individual behaviors, and the structural and ideological drivers of environmental impacts. We will explore environmental sociologists' attempts to understand how these drivers are related. Theoretical, qualitative, and quantitative studies all play important roles in this work.

Global Drivers: Beyond Population Growth

If you are in the environmental field, when people ask you about your profession they might also express some of their own opinions about the drivers of environmental problems. In certain cases, you may hear statements such as "It's about population growth" or "It's a problem of overpopulation." As far back as Thomas Malthus's *Essay on the Principle of Population* (1789), people have feared that human population growth beyond certain levels could lead to resource shortages and societal collapse. Garrett Hardin's (1968) famous narrative about the "tragedy of the commons" also illustrated how overpopulation causes overuse, environmental degradation, and can undermine sustainability. The "tragedy" is that more and more people using a finite shared resource results in overuse and degradation. The same narrative can be applied to explain pollution: too many people using energy and resources causes increasing levels of pollution. This can be applied to carbon emissions and global climate change as well: global warming is occurring because too many people are polluting with carbon. Thus, overpopulation is the culprit. The solution in each case is reducing human population growth, or population control, and some people may even call for a total reduction in the global population to address problems such as climate change. However, as we will explore here, the drivers of our environmental crisis are more complicated than simplified narratives focused only on population growth, and there are serious ethical issues associated with approaches focused on population.

Countering oversimplified Malthusian explanations, natural scientists, human ecologists, and environmental sociologists have contributed to a much more nuanced understanding of the drivers of environmental impacts. It is true that if environmental impacts are caused by the cumulative behaviors of individuals—for example, cutting down trees or driving cars—then the more people doing these activities, the greater the environmental impact. Population size clearly plays a role—but it is not *the* driver of environmental impacts. Ecologists in the 1960s proposed the IPAT equation to provide a more complex understanding of the drivers of environmental impacts. The equation posits that environmental Impact = Population × Affluence × Technology. This equation recognizes that while population plays a role in impacts, so do affluence and technology. In other words, *what people do* in terms of production/consumption and technology can be just as important as *how many people* there are. In addition, it reveals that drivers of impacts are not equally distributed: populations from rich countries have greater impacts.

Drawing from human ecology, environmental sociologists extended IPAT to develop the STIRPAT model, which introduced *stochasticity*. In other words, the coefficients of the drivers are elastic and can change. In a series of publications, Thomas Dietz and Eugene Rosa (1994, 1997) and later Richard York (York et al. 2002, 2003a,b) introduced and applied the STIRPAT model. In this model, T (technology) is conceptualized as including additional factors such as institutions, policy, culture, and social structure, that are not captured in the terms A (affluence) and P (population) (Dietz 2017). STIRPAT has been applied to examine drivers of carbon emissions, sulfur dioxide emissions, fertilizer consumption, and pesticide use, among others (see York and Dunlap 2019). While in many cases population remains a strong influence, quantitative studies applying STIRPAT continue to reveal the significant importance of affluence, measured as Gross Domestic Product (GDP) per capita, as a primary driving force of environmental impacts.

Research has shown that GDP growth is highly correlated with carbon emissions and biodiversity loss. Kyle Knight and Juliet Schor (2014) found a significant positive correlation for both territorial carbon emissions within a country and emissions based on consumption: "for territorial emissions, the coefficient of economic growth is 0.622 ($p < .01$), and for consumption-based emissions the coefficient is 0.895 ($p < .01$)" (Schor 2015: 529). Other studies have found that a GDP growth of 1 percent equals a 0.6 percent growth in material use (Wiedmann et al. 2015) and a 1 percent increase in GDP equals a 0.5–0.7 percent increase in carbon emissions (Burke et al. 2015). In addition, the most notable carbon emissions reductions have occurred during economic recessions due to a reduction in production and consumption (Feng et al. 2015). In terms of biodiversity loss, studies reveal a strong positive association between GDP growth and species endangerment (Czech et al. 2012, Sol 2019). This evidence indicates that economic growth in terms of GDP growth may be a major driver of the environmental crisis.

Identifying economic growth as a major driver of environmental impacts has important implications. GDP measures the monetary value of all goods and services produced in a given time period. Therefore, the relationship between GDP and environmental impact is due to the energy and materials used to produce increasing amounts of goods and services. While increasing levels of production can be interpreted as driven by increased demand from population growth, this explanation overlooks important evidence. The materials and energy produced *per person* continues to increase. Global material production has quadrupled since 1970, growing twice as fast as the human population (Ghosh 2020). In other words, production is not increasing to meet the needs of a growing world population, but is increasing faster than population growth, resulting in more production per person. While in some places needs are not being met, many people in wealthy countries are buying more and more goods and services each year. Yet evidence indicates that this high level of consumption is not improving lives (Easterlin et al. 2010). For example, countries such as Costa Rica have a lower GDP per capita than the US or the UK, but have higher social indicators (including healthy life expectancy, life satisfaction, education, income, employment, equality, and social support) and lower biophysical impacts (O'Neill et al. 2018). Why then do so many countries prioritize GDP growth? This can be partially explained by the power of those who benefit the most from GDP growth: 82 percent of global wealth is going to one percent of the global population (Oxfam 2018).

As we will explore in more depth in the next chapter, due to the implications of associated solutions, the role of economic growth as a major driver of environmental impacts remains a highly contentious topic. There are those who believe that significant environmental impacts emerge during the early stages of economic development and can be addressed with technological and efficiency advances as development continues. Thus, the solution is more economic growth and development. In contrast, those who believe that economic growth will always result in environmental harm argue for a different set of solutions. Others contend that it is actually the entire socioeconomic system, not just economic growth, that needs to be altered to address the drivers of environmental impacts. In other words, the driver is not only GDP growth but the organization of our economic and social system, the system that drives GDP growth. These different positions are informed by specific social theories that we will discuss in this chapter and the next. These theories shape the identification of drivers as well as support for specific solutions. While we will save an in-depth analysis of solutions until the next chapter, it is important to recognize that the implications of certain solutions continue to shape the diagnosis of drivers, as well as resistance to the diagnosis of specific drivers.

Public Sociology: Identifying Drivers of Carbon Emissions

Environmental sociologists have made important contributions to understanding the social drivers of the climate crisis. Identifying the major drivers of carbon emissions is a prerequisite to being able to most effectively mitigate climate change. Richard York's (2012b) work identifies asymmetrical relationships between economic growth and carbon emissions; it was published in *Nature Climate Change* and discussed in *The Washington Post*. While economic growth is associated with more carbon emissions, during economic downturns the decline in emissions is not equal to periods of growth. Andrew Jorgenson, Juliet Schor, and Xiaorui Huang's (2017) research reveals relationships between income inequality and carbon emissions in the US: greater inequality is associated with greater carbon emissions. Their work was featured in *Nature* and received widespread media coverage. In addition, Jared Fitzgerald, Schor, and Jorgenson (2018) identify positive relationships between working hours and carbon emissions; this finding was featured in *The Guardian*, National Public Radio, and *New Scientist*. These studies indicate that economic growth, economic inequality, and working hours are correlated with carbon emissions, with important implications for identifying solutions to the climate crisis.

In 2017 Jorgenson, Schor, York and others participated in a government-funded interdisciplinary workshop focused on social science and climate change. This workshop resulted in comprehensive, policy-oriented publications identifying social drivers of climate change as well as the complex relationships between drivers (Fiske et al. 2018, Jorgenson et al. 2019). Presented in clear and policy-relevant language, these publications summarize research from different social science disciplines on the drivers of climate change. The authors discuss how economic growth is associated with increasing carbon emissions and the role of individual consumption, consumer practices, and lifestyle choices, as well as the significant carbon emissions from the military. Finally, they also discuss the role of power and inequality: those with great wealth use a position of power to maintain their status, and countries benefiting from unequal exchange use power to sustain advantages. Understanding these relationships, and clearly communicating them in useful formats, remains essential for identifying the most effective and just climate change solutions. While this type of work is time-consuming and does not always result in academic publications, it remains critical to inform solutions to the climate crisis.

We can also empirically examine global drivers of environmental impacts by analyzing the ecological footprints of nations. The *ecological footprint* is a representation of the impacts of total consumption (per individual, household, city or nation), measured as the land area used to produce resources and absorb waste. In other words, it is the land area impacted by the environmental stresses associated with consumption. The measure originated in the natural sciences, but has been used by environmental sociologists to examine drivers of environmental impacts. Dietz, Rosa, and York (2007) applied the STIRPAT model to identify drivers of national ecological footprints and found that population and affluence play key roles, and that increasing affluence globally will have an especially substantial impact on the global ecological footprint. A 2019 study focused on the drivers of ecological footprints among African nations reveals that demographics as well as economic and environmental factors shape nations' ecological footprints (which are all relatively low) in ways that are consistent with the STIRPAT model (Denny and Marquart-Pyatt 2019). In addition to examining drivers of total ecological footprints, impacts can be broken down to examine impacts on specific land uses as well as carbon emissions (the carbon footprint). What the ecological footprint highlights is that certain countries and populations in the world consume much more resources than others, and therefore have much higher ecological footprints. For example, according to the Global Footprint Network (2019), countries such as the US, Canada, Australia, and the UK have ecological footprints over eight times higher than most countries in Africa.

World systems theory also guides studies examining global inequities, including inequities in ecological footprints. World systems theory was initially proposed by Immanuel Wallerstein (1974) and explains patterns of resource exploitation and inequality at a global scale. Countries are categorized as either a "core" country associated with colonization and exploitation (the taking of resources and labor for economic growth), or they are categorized as a "peripheral" or "semi-peripheral" country that experiences the loss of resources and labor as well as environmental degradation. If we examine ecological footprints across nations, we find that "core" countries have much higher ecological footprints than peripheral countries (Jorgenson 2003, Jorgenson et al. 2005). In terms of climate change, the Global North or "core" countries have also contributed much more carbon emissions than countries in the Global South (Jorgenson et al. 2019). In other words, affluent populations consume more resources and energy and represent a much more significant driver of environmental impacts. The related concept of "ecologically unequal exchange" also reveals how increasing levels of production and consumption in the Global North disrupt infrastructures, ecosystems, and social systems in the Global South for the purpose of extractive development and export (Givens et al. 2019).

Also illustrating the importance of a world systems perspective, there are clear cases where the consumption of rich countries in the Global North has driven regional environmental degradation in the Global South. Thomas Rudel spent decades studying drivers of deforestation in the tropics, a cause of both the biodiversity and climate crises. Early theorists posited that population growth was driving smallholder farmers deeper into the rainforest, cutting down more and more trees to increase cropland and feed growing local populations. However, what Rudel and colleagues (2009) found instead was that since 1985 the greatest driver of deforestation in the tropics has been the expansion of global markets, primarily the production of beef cattle and soybeans to be exported to countries in the Global North. In other words, deforestation in the tropics has not been driven by increasing local population densities, but by increasing demand for products in the Global North. This illustrates how pressures from far-away sources, such as foreign companies and global markets, can drive regional environmental degradation. As explained by Rudel (2016), the expansion of global markets and agribusiness in the 1980s resulted in the rapid development of new agricultural lands in the tropics, as policies and economic goals encouraged beef and soybean production for export markets. In many cases, large agribusiness companies participated in "land-grabs" and were responsible for deforestation, not local populations. In summary, drivers of environmental impacts can often be traced to far-away actors in affluent "core" countries that continue to use the most resources globally.

The drivers of our environmental impacts are much more complicated than explanations focused solely on human population growth. Affluence, in terms of GDP per capita, continues to drive impacts, as people from wealthy countries consume more energy and resources over time. The disparity in global responsibility for environmental harm is important to consider in terms of environmental and social justice. In addition, oversimplified explanations that blame population growth are largely focused on countries in the Global South, where populations are growing the fastest, such as India and Nigeria. These explanations overlook the fact that impacts per person in these countries remain much less than in the Global North. When people talk about population as a problem, it is important to ask *which population* they are talking about. In terms of carbon emissions, reducing consumption levels in the Global North would have a much greater mitigation impact than reducing population in the Global South. In other words, in the Global South "growth threatens global climate stability less than wealthy nations' consumption practices do"—this is because the wealthiest 10 percent of the global population contribute approximately 36 percent of carbon emissions and the carbon footprint of the elite is 14 times greater than the lowest income group (Jorgenson et al. 2019: 6).

In addition, focusing on population growth as a primary driver of environmental impacts can be dangerous in terms of what solutions are proposed. A 2018 *Vox* article by environmental journalist David Roberts offers a straightforward justification for avoiding a focus on population. Roberts explains that naming "population" as a problem has in many cases resulted in proposed solutions rooted in racism, xenophobia, and eugenics. In other words, strategies have focused on *particular populations*. For example, there have been tragic cases where population control programs resulted in the forced sterilization of minority and low-income women. Roberts argues that talking about population as a driver is dangerous and unnecessary, as programs encouraging female literacy and education (which reduce birth rates) can be implemented without even discussing overpopulation, avoiding the dangers of strategies that might target specific populations or result in unethical outcomes. While population growth plays a role in increasing environmental impacts, beyond female empowerment, approaches focused on population have the potential to be unjust and in violation of human rights. As we will discuss in the next chapter focused on solutions, reducing production and consumption in places where people have more resources than necessary is a less risky and more ethical approach.

Individual and Household Drivers

Other explanations of drivers of environmental impacts focus on individual behaviors. Individuals make choices each day about the products they consume and about their housing and transportation, all of which have environmental impacts. In theory, it is the role of government to create, encourage, or mandate behaviors or behavioral restrictions to protect the environment from significant degradation. For example, in many places, individual littering or the dumping of toxic waste is against the law. Yet for other more indirect or diffuse sources of pollution and environmental degradation, individuals may have some degree of freedom to make choices that can have more or less environmental impact. It is important to acknowledge, however, that the degree of freedom and the ability to make low-impact choices varies depending on an individual's circumstances, opportunities, and constraints.

When we talk about high-impact individual behaviors, what are we talking about? Some behaviors have direct and immediate impacts. For example, if you own a forested piece of land and you cut down the forest, this has immediate environmental impacts and contributes to carbon emissions and habitat loss. If you drive an hour each way to work every day, these carbon emissions add up to contribute to global warming. But other impacts occur from a distance or are indirect and harder to see. For example, if you use a large amount of paper products, trees somewhere are being cut down to make those products. Household use of energy for heat, light, and appliances also adds up to considerable carbon emissions from power plants far away. Consumption choices (*what* we buy) as well as the extent of total consumption (*how much* we buy and *how much* energy we use) all contribute to environmental impacts.

What makes some people adopt more high-impact behaviors than others? First, location matters. If you live somewhere like the US or the UK, you live in a society where high material and energy living is the norm and has been built into your daily life through existing infrastructure. If you live in rural Malawi, your daily impacts are likely much lower. For those who can choose to make higher- or lower-impact choices, what influences those choices? Environmental sociologists, as well as other social and behavioral scientists, have explored what influences environmentally significant behaviors. These behaviors include activism, other forms of public support for environmental protection, and consumption (Stern 2000). Consumption involves the purchase of goods or services, the use and upkeep of goods, waste disposal, and the selection of goods or services specifically to reduce impacts (green consumerism). As explained by Paul Stern (2000: 410), "the environmental impact of any individual's personal behavior, however, is small. Such individual behaviors have environmentally significant impact only in the aggregate, when many people independently do the same things."

Specific theories have been used to guide research on environmentally significant behaviors (Stern 2000). For example, the theory of planned behavior has been used to understand how attitudes, norms, and perceived impact result in intention and behavior. Value-norms-beliefs theory focuses on how specific values inform beliefs that result in personal norms and associated behaviors. Finally, norm activation theory focuses on awareness of consequences and notions of responsibility that activate norms and behaviors. In addition, the social context and culture of the individual remains an important influence (Markle 2019). Different approaches can be used to understand drivers of environmental impacts at the individual or household level, as well as pro-environmental behaviors. Understanding what influences pro-environmental behaviors is important in terms of designing interventions to shape behaviors in ways that can reduce environmental impacts, approaches we will discuss in the next chapter.

Understanding individual and household consumption sociologically is complicated yet critical. Why do people consume environmentally harmful products and *so many* products in general? A sociology of consumption has revealed the importance of class and "conspicuous consumption" as a way for individuals to demonstrate their wealth (Veblen 2005). In other words, certain items are purchased because they represent a high class status. These decisions are shaped by a system of advertising and marketing to encourage higher and higher levels of personal consumption (Schor 2018). Consumption is also linked to identity, as purchases are used to represent and symbolize aspects of personal identity. Individual as well as group identities remain important influences on environmentally significant behaviors (Dietz and

Whitley 2018). In addition, mass/excess consumption is reproduced in society through ritual, relationships, and mass ignorance about associated impacts (Boström 2020).

Many people focus specifically on consumers as drivers of environmental harm because of widespread individualism, especially in the US. For example, through the lens of individualism, climate change is a result of the cumulative actions of many people all contributing carbon emissions. Some of the most significant carbon contributions from individuals come from eating meat and dairy products, electricity and heat, and personal transportation. According the University of Michigan's carbon footprint factsheet (Center for Sustainable Systems 2019), food accounts for 10 to 30 percent of household carbon emissions, with beef and dairy products having the largest contribution. Despite the high impacts of these foods, they are still widely purchased and consumed, especially in wealthy nations. While actual responsibility is difficult to quantify, based on the mitigation potential of individual actions (see next chapter), carbon emissions from the behaviors of individuals remain small compared to industrial, commercial, government/military, and systemic sources. As fossil fuel companies increasingly support apps and other ways to track personal carbon emissions, these individual-focused strategies are increasingly identified in news and social media as purposeful distractions, diverting attention away from the biggest emitters and the systemic changes necessary.

Just as countries with higher GDPs tend to have higher carbon emissions (Knight et al. 2017), wealthier individuals emit more carbon. The "super-rich" who constitute the wealthiest 1 percent of the world population may contribute up to 175 times more carbon emissions than those in the poorest 10 percent (Oxfam 2015). Jorgenson, Schor, and Huang (2017) quantitatively examined relationships between income and carbon emissions in the US and found that "a 1 percent increase in the income share of the top 10 percent from 1997 to 2012 is associated with a 0.606 percent increase in emissions." They also found a positive relationship between higher concentrations of income at the top 5 percent and 1 percent and increased carbon emissions. They conclude that the spending ability of the very wealthy increases carbon-intensive consumption choices. A 2020 study found that the wealthiest 10 percent globally consume 20 times as much energy as the bottom 10 percent, and for transportation the wealthiest 10 percent consume 187 times as much as the bottom 10 percent (Oswald et al. 2020). One explanation of this trend is that as individuals become wealthier they travel more and spend more on luxury transportation options (e.g., vacations, cruises) and energy-intensive goods (cars, boats, planes). Ivanova and Wood (2020) analyzed European households and found that the wealthiest 10 percent account for 27 percent of the EU's carbon footprint, with the most significant contributions from air travel. Another study on household energy use found that wealthier Americans emit approximately 25 percent more carbon emissions, primarily because they have larger homes (Goldstein et al. 2020). Thus, expensive goods, homes, and travel are significant contributors.

Individual and household behaviors, especially for the very wealthy, do add up to contribute to environmental impacts. However, these decisions are not made in a bubble, and are highly influenced by the socioeconomic system in which we live. We become accustomed to routines and norms in our lives that continue to contribute to environmental harm. Environmental sociologists have used practice theory, specifically related to Pierre Bourdieu's concept of habitus (e.g., Carfagna et al. 2014) and Michel Foucault's notion of discipline (e.g, Stuart and Houser 2018) to illustrate how, even in situations where we believe we have free choice, there are often forces we overlook that restrict our options and encourage certain outcomes. *Habitus* refers to how individuals internalize the social order through their thoughts, actions, and relationships (Bourdieu 1977). In other words, individuals are socialized to conform to the social order. In the US especially, people are "disciplined" to adopt a high-consumption society through mass advertising, status, and purchasing norms. Individuals live in a system that continues to encourage certain behaviors and constrain others, resulting in an increase in overall environmental impacts. Thus, it is critical to examine drivers related to the priorities, organization, and the overall structure of our social system.

Public Sociology: Confronting Consumer Culture and Materialism

Why do people, especially in the US, work longer and longer hours to buy more and more things that harm the environment and fail to make them happy? Juliet Schor's books *Plenitude: The New Economics of True Wealth* (2010 with K. White) and *Born to Buy: The Commercialized Child and the New Consumer Cult* (2014) provide explanations of high-consumption, high-impact living, as well as alternative economic and social relations that can result in more positive outcomes. As more and more people work longer hours to pay for more and more unnecessary things, there is an epidemic of unhappiness, debt, and environmental crises. Schor's work has been widely read, as it remains relevant for everyone living in a high-consumption culture and helps to identify more positive alternatives.

Schor has also remained active in working to address overconsumption through working with the Better Future Project and the Center for a New American Dream. The Center for a New American Dream works to expose and counter the drivers of overconsumption and guide people toward a lower-impact and more meaningful and fulfilling way of life. Due to the high social relevance of this work, Schor has been interviewed by many journalists and featured in a wide range of articles and films. Although "more is better" remains the dominant paradigm in many wealthy countries, Schor's message that "less is more" continues to help fuel movements promoting minimalism, simple living, sharing, degrowth, and other efforts aiming to prioritize social and ecological well-being over profit and economic growth.

Structural Drivers

While certain social factors, including economic growth and consumption, are associated with increased environmental degradation, many argue that the underlying driver is larger than any one factor and is related to our social structure. *Social structure* refers to the way society is organized and functions as a system. This includes modes of production and consumption, legal and political institutions, and the underlying motivations shaping the social order. The role of the state in creating policies and managing economies is key in structural analysis, as well as the type of economy, power dynamics, class, labor, and politics. These aspects of the social order are often lumped together into the term *political economy*. Different social theories describe the structural drivers of environmental impacts. The majority of structural analysis in environmental sociology has been inspired by the theories and writings of Karl Marx.

In the mid and late 1800s Karl Marx, as well as his colleague Friedrich Engels, extensively critiqued the dominant social order—industrialized capitalism—and exposed how it was causing social and ecological harm. While both scholars were German, they met in England and their work was heavily influenced by the labor conditions they witnessed in Manchester, a center of manufacturing and industry. They witnessed tragic outcomes related to child labor, low wages, long working hours, unsafe working conditions, and the overall degraded and alienated existence of laborers. In addition, Marx also wrote about the impacts the social order was having on ecosystems and the environment. More than any of the other classical social theorists, Marx explicitly discussed how the capitalist social order, organized to maximize profits for manufacturers and the elite, impacted nature in harmful ways.

According to Marxist theory, the structure of society revolves around the production of materials, and in capitalism this is done for the purpose of accumulating profit. Exchange is based on profits rather than on the satisfaction of human needs or on equity. While there are many definitions of capitalism, it is largely described as a system dominated by private property, wage labor, competition, distinctive classes, the primacy of profit maximization and wealth accumulation, and ever-increasing levels of production and consumption to maintain increasing levels of economic growth. In such a system, nature and workers are often seen and treated as cogs in the production system, or commodities supplying materials and labor. In both cases, degradation is an outcome. Due to competition, debt, and the underlying goals of increasing profits and economic growth, this system is using more and more energy and resources every year—accelerating production and consumption for profit. Marxist theory is critical of capitalism, focusing on outcomes such as social injustice as well as environmental degradation. Environmental sociologists have applied and further developed the work of Marx and other Marxist theorists to explicitly examine the drivers of environmental impacts.

The Treadmill of Production (ToP) theory is grounded in the work of Marx and focuses on how the goal of ever-increasing profit accumulation drives production, consumption, and increasing negative impacts to the environment. As introduced by Allan Schnaiberg (1980) and elaborated by Schnaiberg and Kenneth Gould (1994) and Gould and colleagues (2004), the ToP remains one of the most influential social theories describing the drivers of environmental impacts. The ToP posits that as firms invest in technology to replace labor, they need to increase production and profits to cover the costs. Investment and debt result in an accelerating treadmill of higher and higher levels of production to cover costs. In other words, firms become locked in to accelerating levels of production in order to stay competitive. Increasing production depends on more *withdrawals* from the environment (resource extraction) as well as *additions* to the environment (pollution), therefore increasing environmental impacts. As described by Schnaiberg (1980), most governments largely function in support of the treadmill and encourage increasing levels of production and consumption and economic growth. For example, economic growth has been an explicit policy goal of governments in countries like the US since the 1950s. ToP theory highlights how capitalist systems are growth-dependent and continue to use more and more resources and create more and more waste in order to keep the treadmill accelerating.

ToP theory is useful for understanding how increasing production drives consumption. While there is indeed a production-consumption treadmill, in most cases it is production driving consumption rather than consumer demand driving production (Schnaiberg 1980). To increase economic growth and profits, firms must increase production. They must also increase the sales of their products, using advertising and marketing to create demand. Hence the data on material production per person, quadrupling since 1970 (Circular Economy 2020), supports this description of increasing consumption *per person*—not based on need, but in response to manufactured demand from producers. This has been described as a *dependence effect* (Galbraith 1958), where increasing output demands the creation of desire for consumption—thus production drives increasing levels of consumption. For example, total US expenditures on advertising rose to over $205 billion annually in 2017 (Griner 2017). In addition, the US government continues to allow widespread advertising and advertising aimed at children (which was restricted prior to 1984), while subsidizing industries and encouraging consumption to stimulate economic growth. Thus, evidence also illustrates that the state (especially in the US) operates in support of economic growth and wants citizens to be avid consumers. As we will examine further in the next chapter, because most consumers have limited power to influence firms, solutions must involve confrontations with government, industry, and vested interests.

The ToP theory also continues to reveal how a focus on individual companies or CEOs remains shortsighted in a system that continues to push all CEOs and firms to accelerate production, despite the environmental and social impacts. While people often blame these impacts on specific "greedy" individuals, these explanations overlook the systemic driver of "greedy" decisions—being locked into the ToP. In an accelerating production system prioritizing profits and growth, replacing "greedy" individuals in most cases will result in their replacements making similar decisions. Without regulation, companies are unlikely to invest resources in preventing environmental harm that might impair competition and profits. In addition, companies resist regulation to maintain profits. Cordner (2016) draws from ToP theory to explain how some industries prevent the regulation of toxic chemicals: companies avoid regulation to maximize profits, each year creating more products in a "toxic treadmill."

Insightful and novel applications of ToP theory abound in environmental sociology. For example, a "nanotechnology treadmill" describes how companies and states are driven to prioritize development science over impact science, accelerating nanotech production despite unknown risks to public health and the environment (Gould 2015). Allen, Longo, and Shriver (2018) apply the ToP to illustrate how government bodies, even at a local level, favor strategies that increase economic growth over strategies for environmental protection. The concept of the "treadmill of destruction" has also been used to describe the relationship between military activities and environmental harm, including carbon emissions (Clark et al. 2010, Clark and Jorgenson 2012, Jorgenson and Clark 2016). This "treadmill of destruction" can be increasingly seen in the Global South, where power asymmetries and strong military forces result in the most vulnerable populations facing the bulk of environmental risks and casualties (Givens et al. 2019). Lastly, Simpson, Dunlap, and Fullerton (2019) introduce the "treadmill of information": another example of how the ToP continues to diversify, expanding into new forms.

Environmental sociologists have also used the work of Marx to explain how capital accumulation imperatives disrupt biophysical cycles and can undermine production systems. Marx's discussion of metabolism and the inherent contradictions of capitalism have both been applied to better understand the structural drivers of environmental issues. John Bellamy Foster (1999) offers a detailed understanding of Marx's conception of the metabolic rift, which focused on agricultural soil fertility. Marx described how transforming agriculture into a capitalist endeavor led to soil degradation, as increasing food production for urban populations caused a biophysical rift in terms of the separation of nutrients. Nutrients in the form of food were sent from the countryside to the cities, so the nutrients were not returned to the soils—in a sense "robbing the soil," or more broadly, the "robbery of nature" (Foster and Clark 2018). The pursuit of profit drove this "robbery" until the soil was degraded and food production undermined. Hence, a contradiction emerged between maximizing profits and the biophysical requirements of soil fertility for food production. In what James O'Connor (1988) describes as the "second contradiction of capitalism," capitalism results in supply-side crises as negative environmental impacts eventually undermine the conditions of production. Marx and Engels argued that the contradictions of capitalism resulted in environmental degradation not only in terms of soil fertility, but also through the devastating effects of deforestation and coal mining (Foster 1999). Thus negative environmental impacts are contradictory, as they threaten to undermine production and, in the case of our accelerating environmental crisis, threaten our social and ecological systems.

The concepts of metabolism and the metabolic rift have been widely applied to describe how capitalism is the primary driver of many environmental problems. Many actions to prioritize profit disrupt and alter biophysical cycles. As reordering the world for capitalism increasingly involves changes in biophysical cycles, more and more "rifts" in these cycles continue to emerge. Metabolic rift theory has been applied to understanding how reshaping carbon metabolism for capital accumulation has disrupted carbon cycles, with carbon being extracted and burned faster than it is sequestered, resulting in global climate change (Clark and York 2005). In addition, the overharvesting of fish disrupts marine food chains and ecosystems and creates an oceanic rift (Clausen and Clark 2005). This results in "the tragedy of the commodity," where the commodification of a resource (e.g., fisheries) to be sold for profit drives overexploitation and rifts, not overuse based on population or need (Longo and Clausen 2011; Longo et al. 2015). Foster and Clark (2018: 16) also describe metabolic rifts in our own bodies: "just as the profit-driven capital system disrupts natural processes and cycles, it creates corporeal rifts, undermining general health, the bodily metabolism, and longevity." All of these rifts can be seen as a part of a larger global or planetary rift that increasingly threatens human existence (Foster et al. 2011). According to eco-Marxists, these contradictions will continue to drive environmental impacts and ultimately result in a crisis of capitalism, when production systems (as well as social and ecological systems) are undermined by environmental degradation (Foster 2013).

Public Sociology: Exposing and Politicizing Structural Drivers

John Bellamy Foster continues to be a strong voice maintaining that the capitalist system is the primary driver of environmental impacts. As a Marxist scholar, Foster has illustrated how the capitalist system is fundamentally at odds with ecological sustainability and how, because of widening metabolic rifts and overlooked and ignored contradictions, we are heading deeper into ecological crisis. Foster has published extensively, is the editor of *Monthly Review*, and continues to give talks and interviews for the media and diverse public audiences. This work has important implications for addressing environmental issues, especially the climate crisis.

Foster's work continues to influence the climate movement, supporting calls for "system change, not climate change." In a 2019 *Monthly Review* article, Foster highlighted the IPCC's call for system change, Extinction Rebellion's acts of civil disobedience, Greta Thunberg's speech at the United Nations, the Fridays for Future school strikes, the Sunrise Movement's political mobilization in the US, and proposals for a Green New Deal. Foster also outlined what could make a Green New Deal into a "revolutionary reform," significantly altering the social order to address climate change as well as social injustice. In a 2020 interview about the climate crisis and the Covid-19 pandemic, Foster stated, "we must respond to the dangers to human existence in the 21st century by changing the system, creating a different form of social metabolic reproduction. There is no other way" (Heron 2020). While we are far from having an eco-socialist system (see Chapter 4), Foster continues to write critically about capitalism and the structural drivers of the climate crisis, supporting efforts to push the climate movement to focus on the system, rather than on technological fixes and minor reforms.

In many cases, empirical studies support the ToP and metabolic rift theory. For example, the relationship between increasing GDP and environmental impacts—such as carbon emissions and biodiversity loss, among others—supports the explanation that a growth-dependent capitalist system is problematic and harmful. The significant influence of affluence, economic growth, and increasing levels of production and consumption remain well supported. Only a few examples are highlighted here. York, Rosa, and Dietz (2003a) used the STIRPAT model to analyze greenhouse gas emissions and found that affluence drives emissions as well as urbanization and industrialization, supporting the ToP and metabolic rift theses. Besek and McGee (2014) used cross-national data to illustrate positive relationships between economic growth, urban development, and invasive species, supporting the ToP as a driver of the biodiversity crisis. Jorgensen and Clark (2016) analyzed cross-national data and found a positive relationship between military expenditures and carbon emissions, supporting the "treadmill of destruction." As we will explore in more depth in the following chapter, this evidence has important implications for identifying solutions to environmental problems. If the capitalist system itself is a driver of environmental problems, do we need a new system? Or is there a way to use technology and human innovation to "green" capitalism and make it less harmful?

An increasing number of environmental sociologists have applied the work of Karl Polanyi (1944) to understand structural drivers of environmental impacts. Polanyi explained how commodification and market expansion could be destructive forces in society, and specifically how markets created for the "false commodities" of land, labor, and money would result in disastrous consequences without adequate social protections. In recent decades, we have experienced a rapid expansion in the commodification of nature through development, privatization, and the creation of new markets (Burawoy 2015). Many of the negative impacts of market expansion described by Polanyi can be seen today as a result of the rise of neoliberalism and the rollback of regulations protecting people and the environment (Brechin and Fenner 2017). Polanyi's work supports the argument that markets are only appropriate in certain cases and with protective measures, and that social and environmental well-being should be prioritized before profit and market-logic (Kaup 2015). Polanyi's concept of *embeddedness* illustrates how, historically, economic systems existed as subordinate to social goals and relationships. With the expansion of markets, economic rationality became so dominant that many social values and goals became subordinate to wealth accumulation. This has important implications for understanding the drivers of the climate crisis, as the commodification of nature, market expansion, and overall attempts to embed both society and nature within the economic system have contributed to global warming (Kaup 2015, Stuart et al. 2019). Marx and Polanyi criticized the capitalist system and identified fundamental flaws, yet they expressed divergent ideas about the root problems and solutions. In both cases, their structural explanations help to reveal underlying relationships and the systemic drivers of environmental impacts.

The Role of Ideology

While constructionist perspectives are important for understanding the social dimensions of environmental impacts, they are also important for understanding the social drivers of impacts. Again, we find that *ideas matter*. Ideologies shape and are shaped by the structural drivers of environmental impacts. Ideology refers to an individual's worldview, or general beliefs about what exists, what is good and bad, and what is possible (Therborn 1980). People often discuss political ideology. For example, *neoliberal ideology* refers to a general belief in individualism, personal freedom, private property, free markets (market fundamentalism), and small government. A hegemonic ideology is socially dominant, becoming common-sense and taken for granted; it may persist until another ideology takes its place (Gramsci 1971). Different ideologies drive material relations with the natural world. Thus, examining ideology is important for understanding drivers of environmental impacts. Schnaiberg (1980) briefly discussed the importance of the ideology of growth in relation to the ToP. In general, social structures shape ideologies and ideologies shape practices and reinforce social structures. A Marxist "negative" conception of ideology focuses on how ideas and practices can mask or obscure the reality of relationships, concealing underlying contradictions (Larrain 1979). In summary, ideologies shape how we view and act toward the nonhuman world, and they also conceal certain realities and serve to maintain social structures.

In a series of articles, Ryan Gunderson (2015, 2016, 2017) illustrates why ideology is important to understand in environmental sociology. Drawing from the critical theory of the Frankfurt School, Gunderson (2015) argues that ToP scholarship and environmental sociology in general would benefit from a deeper understanding of how social psychology and ideology (or ideational forces) shape environmental relations. Contradiction-concealing ideas, expressed in our internal ways of thinking, shared beliefs, and "unreflective" taken-for-granted practices, shape our interactions with the natural world and reinforce specific relations. Certain ways of thinking or rationalities become dominant due to preexisting social relations, including instrumental and economic rationalities (Gunderson 2015). "Domination ideology," for example, refers to the view that the world was created for humans—to be dominated and used as humans see fit. Ideology is not an independent variable; it is always embedded in preexisting social relations.

There are clear connections between ideational forces and structural drivers, as "the domination of nature is an inherent feature of economic growth, [and] ... is maintained by instrumental rationality" (Gunderson 2015). These ideational forces also have real material consequences. For example, early US settlers' views about domination and the taming of wilderness resulted in widespread deforestation. Domination ideology and economic rationality can also help explain the rise of industrial animal agriculture and the biodiversity crisis (Stuart and Gunderson 2020). In addition, ideologies shape technological innovation and use—all of these examples illustrating how ideology is a *material* phenomenon (Gunderson et al. 2019).

Examining the Marxist conception of ideology, and employing critique of ideologies, are critical for understanding "why society continues to degrade the environment despite the fact that it knows it is destroying its life support" (Gunderson 2017: 263). In other words, why do we maintain a social structure that is incompatible with environmental sustainability and our own survival? Examining ideology can help us to understand what keeps the ToP "firmly in place" (Gunderson 2017: 265), despite all that we know about climate change, biodiversity loss, and the relationship to economic growth. Certain ideologies conceal the underlying contradictions of capitalism, legitimizing, reifying, and reproducing the current social order. For example, Gunderson et al. (2018) argue that the idea of "green growth" conceals the inherent contradictions between growth-dependent capitalism and environmental sustainability. Evidence illustrating structural drivers of environmental harm continues to be overlooked or dismissed, based on arguments that the "greening" of growth and technological innovation will save us from escalating environmental impacts. In the face of existential threats, contradiction-concealing ideologies continue to be used by vested interests to maintain power relations and the status quo.

Ideology is also important for understanding how production drives consumption, and more specifically, how it drives harmful levels of unnecessary overconsumption in wealthy countries. As explained by Boström (2020: 2), excess consumption permeates society largely because "expansive capitalism needs the support of an ideology or culture that legitimizes it." Ideology is used to keep people consuming at high rates, rates necessary to keep the ToP accelerating and GDP growing. As observed decades ago by Herbert Marcuse (1964: 246, 12), without increasing levels of consumption, "the established mode of production could not be sustained," therefore individuals are made into super-consumers, "redefined by the rationality of the given system." Much of this ideology is communicated through advertising, convincing people that they need new material products in order to have "the good life," to create specific identities, and to demonstrate social status. The creation of false needs through advertising conceals the underlying reality that overconsumption is for the purpose of wealth accumulation for the few, while the ToP drives us further into environmental crisis. In other words, "the ideology of overconsumption masks the irrationality of the capitalist system of never-ending production, consumption, and destruction" (Stuart et al. 2020: 208).

Seeing the Whole Picture

Identifying the underlying drivers of environmental impacts is a necessary step before we can act to effectively and justly reduce impacts. As illustrated in this chapter, the drivers of environmental degradation are complex and exist across multiple scales. We can examine global data to identify relationships and factors that drive environmental impacts, such as carbon emissions or biodiversity loss. We can also assess what individual behaviors and household practices result in negative environmental impacts. Tying all of these together, structural explanations illustrate the importance of how the system is organized, as well as the ideologies that dominate and maintain the system. In addition, while global analysis might tell us that population and economic growth are the primary drivers of environmental impacts, structural analysis reveals how the current system is growth-dependent and relies on increasing levels of production and consumption per person.

Through combining these perspectives, we get a much more nuanced and in-depth understanding of drivers. As an example, let's look at consumption. At an individual level, quantitative analysis reveals that wealthy people consume more resources and are responsible for more carbon emissions. This is also confirmed at a global scale by studies that find wealthy countries having greater environmental impacts, including carbon emissions. However, we need structural analysis to understand the underlying driver, and why people are consuming so much. While some assume that production is increasing due to demand, we see that production drives consumption through advertising in order to maintain constant growth. We also see how ideology plays an important role, convincing people to consume more and more while concealing who benefits (the wealthiest 1 percent), and obscuring the underlying relationships driving us deeper into environmental crisis. Energy and material use continue to increase for the sake of economic growth and wealth accumulation, but at what social and ecological costs?

Identifying the drivers of environmental impacts has important implications for identifying the appropriate solutions. Certain drivers are overlooked because the associated solutions could negatively impact those who currently benefit from the status quo. There are strong forces actively working to maintain and reproduce the current social structure, despite inherent contradictions. For example, there are vested interests that would rather we not focus on how economic growth is a driver of the climate and biodiversity crises. Whether we realize it or not, ideology is widely used as a tool to distract, conceal, and maintain the status quo. However, in a rapidly escalating state of crisis we must work quickly to expose ideology, identify root drivers, and get to work applying the most effective and just solutions.

Discussion Questions

1. In what ways is focusing on population as the primary driver of environmental impacts oversimplified? What other factors are important?
2. Why is GDP correlated with biodiversity loss, climate change, and other environmental impacts? Why does it keep increasing?
3. What influences individuals' decisions that result in environmental impacts?

4. What is meant by "structural" drivers?
5. How have the concepts of the treadmill of production and the metabolic rift been applied to understand different environmental issues? What are some diverse examples?
6. What is ideology and why does it matter?

Suggested Reading

Bates, D. (2020). Population, demography, and the environment. In *Twenty Lessons in Environmental Sociology*. Edited by K. A. Gould and T. L. Lewis. New York: Oxford University Press.

Boström, M. (2020). The social life of mass and excess consumption. *Environmental Sociology* 6(3): 268–278.

Clark, B., & R. York. (2005). Carbon metabolism: Global capitalism, climate change, and the biospheric rift. *Theory and Society* 34(4): 391–428.

Dietz, T. (2017). Drivers of human stress on the environment in the twenty-first century. *Annual Review of Environment and Resources* 42: 189–213.

Dunlap, R. E., & A. M. McCright. (2011). Organized climate change denial. *The Oxford Handbook of Climate Change and Society* 1: 144–160.

Foster, J. B. (1999). Marx's theory of metabolic rift: Classical foundations for environmental sociology. *American Journal of Sociology* 105(2): 366–405.

Gould, K. A., D. N. Pellow, & A. Schnaiberg. (2004). Interrogating the treadmill of production: Everything you wanted to know about the treadmill but were afraid to ask. *Organization & Environment* 17(3): 296–316.

Gunderson, R. (2017). Ideology critique for the environmental social sciences: What reproduces the treadmill of production? *Nature and Culture* 12(3): 263–289.

Jorgenson, A. K., S. Fiske, K. Hubacek, J. Li, T. McGovern, T. Rick, ... & A. Zycherman. (2019). Social science perspectives on drivers of and responses to global climate change. *Wiley Interdisciplinary Reviews: Climate Change* 10(1): e554.

Pellow, D. 2020. The state and policy: Imperialism, exclusion, and ecological violence as state policy. In *Twenty Lessons in Environmental Sociology*. Edited by K. A. Gould & T. L. Lewis. New York: Oxford University Press.

4
Identifying Solutions

While we can scientifically assess environmental impacts and identify the likely drivers of those impacts, the most challenging task remains identifying and pushing forward effective solutions. In this book, we will not skirt around or shy away from this daunting yet critical task. Understanding the underlying drivers of environmental degradation is key to informing the evaluation of possible solutions. But even with this knowledge, there are a range of solution strategies that can be pursued, which have very different impacts on specific interest groups, races, and classes. Identifying solutions also remains a challenging task due to inherent unknowns and our inability to predict future events and outcomes. Data can inform what is likely going to be an effective solution and it is critical to carefully evaluate this data. Still, uncertainty remains. As a result, part of choosing solution pathways involves acknowledging the risks of different strategies. Some paths are much riskier than others, with vast moral implications. As we face multiple existential threats, we must evaluate which solution pathways will offer the most protection for *all* people and result in the least amount of suffering and loss. Some pathways may offer a future of keeping global warming within 2°C, while others may not. While we will continue to face the impacts of climate change and biodiversity loss into the future, the extent of these impacts depends on the solutions identified and pursued today.

Like drivers of impacts, solutions can be identified and pursued at different scales of influence, with implications for who is responsible for making change happen. Individuals can make choices to change their behaviors, for example, in ways that reduce toxic chemicals, carbon emissions, or consumption in general. Should it be the responsibility of individuals to actively identify and minimize their environmental impacts on a daily basis? While individual behavior change can be important for illustrating how people can live lower-impact lifestyles and reduce the impacts associated with transportation and household consumption, solutions that depend on the cumulative decisions of individuals will only achieve so much. Industries can also choose to make more environmentally friendly choices and use more efficient and less harmful technologies. In addition, governments can play a key role in encouraging and incentivizing changes in households and industries, and could foster a beneficial "modernization" process to reduce impacts through policy reform and technological solutions.

However, empirical studies informed by structural explanations reveal possible limitations, constraints, and contradictions related to these approaches. This calls into question whether individual, technological, and reformist strategies will be enough to minimize impacts or even maintain a planetary system that can support life as we know it. Will these approaches be enough or is it necessary to more fundamentally change the organization and structure of society? What would solutions involving structural change look like? And what are the risks and moral implications associated with these different solution pathways? These are difficult questions to answer, yet they are now critical for environmental sociologists and others to examine. The answers and what we do with those answers have tremendous consequences for the human race and all other species on Earth. There is no time to waste. These difficult questions must be examined, decisions must be made, and solutions must be pushed forward rapidly in order to create the most sustainable and just future possible.

Environmental sociologists continue to play an important role in these discussions through analyzing relevant data, exploring pathways supported by different theoretical positions, and weighing the possible benefits, limitations, risks, and moral implications of different solutions. This work becomes even more important and urgent as we face a narrowing window of time to act to minimize the impacts of climate change and biodiversity loss. Due to the increasing impacts and risks associated with these existential threats, solutions are being increasingly discussed, evaluated, and implemented. As opportunities to push forward solutions emerge, it remains critical that citizens, scholars, and policy-makers have already evaluated the options and identified the most effective, equitable, and ethical pathways forward.

It is important to again acknowledge that identifying solutions in many ways depends on what is identified as the driver of a problem. In other words, the solution depends on how the problem is defined, framed, and understood. If, for example, climate change is seen as a problem caused by the cumulative decisions of individuals, then the solutions would focus on changing individual behaviors. While many people continue to see environmental problems in specific ways that result in a focus on certain types of solutions as *the* answer, here we examine the ways that different solutions can together contribute to addressing environmental impacts, especially those related to our escalating existential threats. In some cases, we do not have to approach solutions through an either/or lens. We can apply multiple approaches to address environmental impacts. We certainly need "all hands on deck" to navigate these tumultuous, uncharted waters. In other cases, certain solution pathways might distract us from more effective alternatives or directly preclude or undermine more effective solutions. Thus, it is critical to identify the potential benefits of proposed solutions as well as the possible limitations and risks. As the environmental crisis intensifies, this work has never been more important.

The Big Picture

We begin with a macro, data-informed, "big picture" perspective. As discussed in the previous chapter, based on the use of STIRPAT and other analyses, certain global-level factors have been identified as increasing environmental impacts. The most significant drivers identified in global-scale analyses are *population* and *affluence* (GDP). For reasons already explained, we will not focus on population beyond acknowledging that policies and programs to support female empowerment, education, and well-being have many benefits, including lower birth rates. In terms of affluence, we know that countries that produce and consume more have higher rates of material and energy use and therefore higher carbon emissions, waste production, and resource use. In the previous chapter, we also saw that in many cases impacts in poorer countries, or peripheral countries, are driven by consumption in wealthy countries, or core countries. Is continual wealth accumulation in these countries necessary? Is it beneficial for well-being?

Environmental sociologists have analyzed global data to help answer these questions. For example, Roberts and others (2020) explain that well-being in terms of life expectancy, literacy rates, and other social indicators is not correlated with affluence, in terms of GDP. In other words, past a certain point, GDP does not increase well-being. Roberts' and others (2020: 2) state: understanding that "human well-being is not identical with economic purchasing power, is essential to addressing the climate crisis." The authors analyzed global data on life expectancy and carbon emissions, finding that there are countries, like Costa Rica, with very high life expectancy and low carbon emissions. The authors argue that this illustrates how we can have high well-being and low carbon emissions, or a good life without overshooting planetary limits. The climate crisis indeed remains the most ominous global environmental threat, with warming increasing each year as we add more and more carbon into the atmosphere. In terms of solutions to this serious crisis, J. T. Roberts and colleagues (2020: 3) explain:

It should be possible to restructure our economic systems so that human needs and quality of life are provided without undermining planetary life support systems ... but this will require facing the powerful forces of highly profitable industries—especially those dependent upon the extraction and processing of fossil fuels.

In other words, at a global level, if economic systems are restructured to prioritize well-being rather than higher and higher levels of production/GDP/affluence, we could be able to address the climate crisis as well as many other environmental issues. This means applying solutions that rein in the global treadmill of production and the associated material and energy use. Yet those who continue to profit from fossil fuels and from increasing levels of production and consumption remain powerful, and are actively working to maintain the current system.

This big-picture narrative is well supported beyond the work of environmental sociologists. Economists, scientists, and environmental activists argue that we are already surpassing the Earth's biophysical limits (e.g., Daly 2013, Steffen et al. 2018). We have already surpassed boundaries related to the nitrogen cycle, biodiversity, and climate (Steffen et al. 2015). Based on the ecological footprint concept, Earth Overshoot Day represents the day each year that humanity uses more resources and services than can be regenerated in a year. This day continues to occur earlier and earlier as more resources and energy are used each year. A growing number of economists also agree that GDP is a problematic indicator of progress and well-being, pushing us beyond planetary limits (e.g., Stiglitz 2009, Victor 2010, Daly 2013, Stiglitz 2019a,b).

Economists and ecological economists increasingly call for the abandonment of GDP growth as the ultimate goal of the economy. They argue that GDP has failed to be a good indicator of well-being and quality of life (e.g., O'Neill 2012, Stiglitz 2019a,b). Alternative indicators, including Gross National Happiness, the Index of Sustainable Economic Welfare, and the General Progress Indicator, also illustrate that GDP remains a poor indicator of social progress in terms of health, education, well-being, and happiness. Nobel Prize winner Joseph Stiglitz has been increasingly vocal about the problems of using GDP as a primary indicator of progress, calling for alternative indicators that better support social and ecological well-being. Stiglitz (2019b) states that "we need better tools to assess economic performance and social progress" and explains that his concerns about GDP "have now been brought to the fore with the climate crisis."

Stigltiz further argues, "if we measure the wrong thing, we will do the wrong thing." Others agree that not only is chasing GDP growth leading us further into environmental crisis, it is preventing human flourishing. As explained by Herman Daly (2013: 24), while it is largely believed that "without economic growth all progress is at an end ... on the contrary, without growth ... true progress finally will have a chance." Ecological economists call for a planned contraction in material and energy use (called *degrowth*), which would result in GDP decline but could also increase well-being (Kallis 2018). Through a reduction in production and consumption to a sustainable steady state, we could maintain a system that meets our needs within planetary boundaries.

Given the original purpose of GDP, and the abundant evidence that increasing GDP is leading us further into crisis, an increasing number of people are questioning increasing GDP as a social goal. In 2019, both New Zealand and Iceland decided to prioritize other indicators of well-being before GDP. This is significant, and other nations are considering similar changes. While some maintain that GDP should still be used as one of many indicators, others argue that it should be abolished altogether and replaced with indicators that are more appropriate. While abandoning GDP growth as the primary goal of the global economy would certainly open up opportunities to better address environmental threats, additional structural changes would be necessary beyond simply changing our indicator of progress.

With this macro view in mind, we now examine a range of solutions at different scales beginning with a focus on individual actions. We will then explore how societies at large can adapt, transition, or transform to a lower-impact state. Is it a matter of cumulative individual choices and new technologies to reduce the impacts of production, or do we need to slow down the treadmill of (over)production? How societies answer these questions will have important consequences. We must keep the moral implications in clear focus, as "everything is at stake" (Klinenberg et al. 2020). In other words, we are at a critical juncture, where identifying the most effective and just solutions and rapidly implementing them is critical to create the most sustainable and just future possible.

Individual Solutions

Individual behavior changes continue to be a primary focus when discussing solutions to environmental problems, especially climate change. In response to the IPCC 1.5°C special report (2018), many news articles focused on what individuals can do to reduce their personal carbon footprints. Individual actions to reduce carbon emissions include using energy-efficient appliances, weatherizing homes, reducing total energy use, installing solar panels, using public transportation or biking, and buying a hybrid or electric vehicle. These actions can add up, and they continue to be promoted. Environmental sociologists and others have helped us to understand how much individual and household actions can reduce environmental impacts, especially in terms of carbon emissions, and what influences these individual actions.

Thomas Dietz and colleagues have made significant contributions toward understanding how individuals and households can help mitigate climate change (see Dietz et al. 2020). In a widely cited study, Dietz and others (2009) found that changes in individual and household energy use could reduce carbon emissions by more than 7 percent in the US. Households are responsible for about 31 percent of US carbon dioxide emissions, equivalent to about 8 percent of global emissions (Dietz et al. 2009). Yet to realize this full potential, it is critical to understand what factors motivate or constrain these behavioral changes (Allen et al. 2015, Dietz 2015). For example, Wolske, Stern, and Dietz (2017) examined what factors influence interest in installing residential solar photovoltaic systems in the US and found that environmental attitudes/interest, perceived benefits, social curiosity, trust, and social networks are all important influences. This type of work not only reveals what drives or restricts behavioral decisions but also how policies and programs can be designed to intervene and encourage lower-energy use or the use of renewable energy sources. For example, Dietz and colleagues

(Vandenbergh et al. 2010, Stern et al. 2010) used data to explore specifically how government programs could be used as a "behavioral wedge" to reduce household energy use.

Beyond reducing household energy use, individuals can adopt a range of other practices to reduce carbon emissions with potential cumulative significance. Researchers estimate that a shift to "green consumption" (choosing lower-impact products) in European countries could reduce carbon emissions by 25 percent (Moran et al. 2018). In a 2018 report, the Center for Behavior and the Environment estimates that the widespread adoption of 30 different behavioral changes could mitigate from 19 to 36 percent of global carbon emissions between 2020 and 2050 (CBE 2018). Based on studies illustrating how the very wealthy are responsible for more carbon emissions (discussed in the previous chapter), reducing consumption, travel, and home size could also reduce carbon emissions. While this could be done voluntarily through personal consumption choices, we will also examine interventions to encourage such behaviors later in this chapter.

Eco-labels and green consumerism continue to be promoted as a way to address environmental issues. For example, if you are concerned about the biodiversity crisis you could buy shade-grown coffee, which supports wildlife habitat and prevents deforestation. A more common form of green consumption is buying organic foods. Certified organic food must meet specific criteria that tend to reduce agricultural pollution and increase protection for biodiversity. The idea behind green consumption is that these choices are a way to "vote with your dollar" and protect the environment through the products we choose (Lorenzen 2014).

However, the effectiveness of green consumerism as a solution has been widely criticized. For example, drawing from Marx's work on commodity fetishism, Gunderson (2014) examines green or ethical consumerism as an approach to address problems and concludes that such approaches reinforce current structural relations that are inherently harmful. In many cases, green consumption as a solution to environmental problems remains limited and is counteracted by increasing levels of overall production and consumption driven by a growth-dependent system. Green consumption can also fuel overconsumption as new "green" products are marketed and purchased to create identity or demonstrate social status. Others argue that reducing total consumption, rather than increasing "green" consumption, would be more impactful, for example, in reducing global carbon emissions (Alfredsson 2004, Boström and Klintman 2019). While some consumers choose green products in an attempt to make a difference "out there" in the environment (e.g., climate change), consumers are also trying to make green choices to protect themselves and their families from harm.

While most governments have environmental laws to protect citizens, in many cases individuals are still responsible for protecting themselves from environmental harm. As discussed in Chapter 2, Ulrich Beck's seminal work *Risk Society* (1992) describes a society of increasing environmental risks due to modernization, technology, and industrialization. Beck argues that these risks require more reflexivity, involving the ability to identify, understand, and address risks as they emerge or even before they are actualized. Reflexivity can relate to scientific expertise, governance, and individual consumer-citizens (Boström et al. 2017). Reflexivity at a societal level will be discussed in the next section. Here, we focus on individual reflexivity and how individuals can attempt to understand, assess, minimize, and avoid environmental risks, focusing on exposure to toxic chemicals.

Due to government commitments to precautionary approaches, European countries have more stringent policies to protect citizens from environmental toxins compared to the US, where it is largely up to individuals to reduce their exposure to toxins present in products. It is often a surprise to people that the US government does not regulate the use of chemicals until substantial evidence of harm has been demonstrated, which is legally challenging to do. Even substances with known toxicity, such as asbestos, are not banned in the US, due to these legal obstacles. When we buy toothpaste, shampoo, lotion, food, or other products in the US, we cannot assume they are free of chemicals that cause cancer, hormone disruption, birth defects, infertility, or nervous system damage. In many cases, products do contain hazardous ingredients and one can discover this upon exploring the Environmental Working Groups' Skin-Deep

Database. There are many toxins that we introduce into our lives every day through the products we use.

Norah MacKendrick's research (2014, 2018) illustrates the challenges and drawbacks to a "precautionary consumption" approach, in which individuals are responsible for risk reduction. This approach relies on consumers to learn about the products they purchase and the possible impacts of the chemicals in these products. This labor largely falls on the shoulders of women, and mothers in particular, who attempt to make choices to reduce the chemical body burdens of their family members. This form of protection has become largely normalized as an expected maternal duty. However, many mothers do not have the time, money, or opportunities to learn about products and/or choose safer products. In *Better Safe than Sorry* (2018), MacKendrick draws from personal interviews with mothers and an analysis of Whole Foods Market to illustrate how women face the challenge of "precautionary consumption" and how class, income, and time limit their abilities to protect their children—widening already existing inequalities. In addition, MacKendrick explains how these individualized approaches can result in choosing ignorance, as people "intentionally ignore information about contamination to maintain a sense of normalcy" (MacKendrick & Stevens 2016). This work reveals the challenges, and possibly the futility, of trying to learn about and avoid ubiquitous environmental chemicals as an individual.

Public Sociology: The Limits of Precautionary Consumption

Norah MacKendrick's work (2014: 708, 2018) is an example of public sociology, as it has "implications for all mothers, but especially those who already exist on the margins of normative motherhood." This work is highly relatable to women's everyday lives, as they struggle to keep their families safe from ever-expanding combinations of harmful chemicals present in everyday products. Because this work is relevant to so many people's lives, it has been discussed in

The Washington Post (2018), which explained how "MacKendrick writes that the current era of deregulation places an undue burden on parents—mostly on mothers—to make complicated choices to ensure that the products and foods they buy are safe for children." MacKendrick's work has also been discussed in *The Guardian* as well as a variety of other media outlets, including National Public Radio.

In terms of policy, MacKendrick's findings illustrate the limitations of individual "precautionary consumption" approaches, and emphasize the need for government regulations and systemic solutions to protect people from toxins. This work contributes important insights not only regarding the limitations of individualized solutions to environmental impacts but also in terms of gender relations, motherhood, and environmental justice. Along with others, MacKendrick brings into question the effectiveness and morality of individualized approaches to environmental risk reduction. As powerful actors and industries continue to oppose more stringent regulations for chemicals in the US, more work is necessary to illustrate the inadequacy of individual attempts to reduce risk and the need for systemic protection from toxins.

Solutions that focus on individual behavior changes through voluntary means are in general more widely supported than approaches in which governments might restrict certain practices or behaviors. A focus on individual solutions, protecting yourself or doing your part to protect the environment, aligns with neoliberal governance and ideology. In governance, this has resulted in the state giving more responsibilities and freedoms to the private sector and individuals, and shrinking government programs, services, and resources. As an ideology, neoliberalism promotes individual liberties and eschews government intervention. Neoliberal ideology and individualism have become naturalized over the past several decades, especially in the US. Individual choice is sacred, and emphasized through a focus on entrepreneurship and consumerism. Thus, in many cases, social problems are framed as individual problems best addressed through individual solutions. In addition, approaches that focus on individuals do not call for systemic change and therefore do not challenge those who benefit from the current system. While there are certainly benefits to individuals making lower-impact choices, it is important to contextualize the broad political support for individual-focused approaches and to question if adhering to this ideological position will result in the most sustainable and just social and ecological outcomes.

There are additional reasons to question the effectiveness of a reliance on individual solutions to address environmental problems. In terms of climate change mitigation through individual behavior change, the Center for Behavior and the Environment (2018) estimates that about two-thirds of all global carbon emissions are linked to either direct or indirect consumption, yet they also state that behavioral change can mitigate only 19 to 36 percent of carbon emissions. This reveals how the majority of emissions related to consumption remain outside of individuals' ability to influence. These uncontrollable factors relate to materials and energy production as well as transportation infrastructure and options. For example, the reduction in global carbon emissions due to the Covid-19 pandemic lockdown was around 17 percent. While some claimed this was great news, and that individual changes can really add up, scientists explained that "at the same time, 83 percent of global emissions are left, which shows how difficult it is to reduce emissions with changes in behaviour … Just behavioural change is not enough" (Harvey 2020).

Based on what we know, it would be beneficial yet insufficient for all of us to adopt behavioral changes to mitigate climate change. It is beneficial to reduce any emissions that we can. It is insufficient because the remaining majority of emissions will still result in over 2°C of warming. Global emissions need to be roughly halved by 2030 and reach net zero by 2050 in order to stay within 1.5°C. Even coordinated individual actions at a massive scale would leave the industries, infrastructures, and production processes that create the majority of emissions intact. In other words, any efforts that leave out the majority of emissions will not be sufficient to limit warming. To address the majority of emissions, larger changes are necessary. While individual consumption and behavioral changes are insufficient, this does not mean they should not be pursued; it means only that we must acknowledge that additional solutions are necessary.

There is also a risk that a focus on individual solutions to climate change can backfire or divert attention away from the need to recreate our energy, transportation, and production-consumption systems. There is some evidence of paradoxical outcomes to green consumerism. One study found that people who bring their own shopping bags to the store have a higher chance of buying unnecessary or "hedonic" items, and another study found that buying green products makes people more likely to steal or cheat (Lowrey 2019). Even more pernicious is a reduction in support for system change. A 2017 study indicates that individual and household actions to reduce carbon emissions can result in reduced support for climate policies, like a carbon tax (Werfel 2017). A 2019 publication titled "Nudging Out Support for a Carbon Tax" illustrates that when individuals are given options to reduce energy use on their own, there is less support for a carbon tax (Hagmann et al. 2019). Overall these studies suggest that, due to human psychology, individual actions to reduce carbon emissions can reduce support for the climate policies necessary to address the majority of emissions. If individuals are lulled into a place of personal satisfaction (e.g., "I have done my part") and a false sense that these actions are enough, it undermines our ability to minimize warming. Some environmentalists suggest that the fossil fuel industry and other vested interests are promoting and funding individual-focused solutions, including creating phone apps that track personal carbon emissions, as a distraction to forestall climate policies that might impact profitability (e.g., Jensen 2009, Byskov 2019).

Other factors also undermine the potential of climate change mitigation through individual behavior change. If there is a potential 10 to 30 percent emissions reduction through individual changes, there are also factors that constrain this potential. A key relationship that undermines the effectiveness of green consumerism is that in most cases production drives consumption through advertising

(Galbraith 1958, Schnaiberg 1980). Therefore, the idea of "consumer sovereignty" is largely a myth. In other words, "buying green" or "voting with your dollar" is not usually a direct or forceful mechanism of social change. In addition, trying to address climate change through consumer-based activism puts individuals up against powerful forces. The current growth-oriented economic system continues to encourage more and more consumption per person, a trend that counteracts efforts to reduce carbon emissions. In many contexts a low-carbon lifestyle goes against the dominant economic and cultural tide and, therefore, a concerned climate citizen must maneuver each day against a forceful high-consumption current. Finally, focusing on individual actions can result in judging and shaming others based on their choices. However, choices in line with being a good climate citizen are not possible for everyone; these depend on their income, location, time, and the options available. Instead of having people struggle to be good climate citizens, we could create a low-carbon system where by default we all have low-carbon lifestyles. But this would require larger-scale solutions. Hence, voting remains an important individual activity to elect leaders who will work to address our environmental crisis and prioritize social and ecological well-being.

Modernization

Beyond the micro-level decisions of individuals, environmental sociologists have also developed different theories about how solutions could emerge at a societal level. Some aspects of these visions seem to complement each other, while others are in contradiction. First, we examine what Fisher and Jorgenson (2019) describe as the more "optimistic" visions of how societies can address environmental impacts. We will examine two visions of modernization: "reflexive modernization" and "ecological modernization." It should be noted that both of these visions of modernization originated in Europe, and that different social and political conditions may make them more possible in a European context. These modernization theories differ in what they focus on as well as the means to achieve solutions.

Reflexive Modernization

Ulrich Beck's (1992) theory of the risk society argues that we can no longer ignore the negative environmental consequences of industry and development, and we must transition to a new form of modernization that acknowledges and addresses these risks. We increasingly face a multitude of risks that are side effects linked to the development of technology and industrialization. Actions come back to haunt us in unforeseen ways: "The agents of modernization themselves are emphatically caught in the maelstrom of hazards that they unleash and profit from" (Beck 1992: 37). Beck highlights the problems with a narrow prioritization of profit and production: "In the effort to increase productivity, the associated risks have always been and still are being neglected" (Beck 1992: 60). He argues that the answer is to stop neglecting these risks and to address them through a process of "reflexive modernization."

Reflexive modernization involves a shift in priorities to increase social protections. In a reflexive society, actions and policies must be reassessed and adapted as needed to address environmental impacts (Beck, 1992, Beck et al., 2003). This societal response is largely driven from the bottom up by concerned citizens and social movements that pressure the state to address risks. Beck highlights the importance of personal and societal self-critique and self-confrontation in order to reshape practices and institutions—questioning how we currently do things and finding safer ways to move forward (Beck 1996). Reflexive modernization is spurred by the growth of individual awareness and actions, the emergence of reflexive social movements, and the rise of "sub-politics" that push forward new worldviews and political agendas (Beck 1992). Thus, social concern pushes the state to create new policies and programs to reduce risks.

Boström and colleagues (2017) revisit the concept of reflexivity in environmental sociology. They argue that reflexivity remains a useful concept in the discipline, yet it more often highlights what is not happening that what ought to happen. In other words, in many cases social actors and organizations are not being reflexive and problems persist or worsen. In other cases, actors may be reflexive but solutions are stymied and problems fail to be addressed. Boström and colleagues (2017: 13) state that "it is questionable whether reflexivity is sufficient in itself as a principle to guide practice towards more sustainability." Thus, reflexivity alone may not be enough. We must also ask additional questions: "What path dependencies are confronting us? Do we have to develop new understandings, roles, and guidelines to avoid reproducing problems? How do our current norms, ways of communicating, and routines prevent our imaginations from seeking and finding better practices?" (Boström et al. 2017: 13).

Another important question is: does reflexive modernization involve only minor reforms, or could it involve a larger systemic transformation? According to Beck (1992), reflexive modernization involves a shift in social priorities that goes beyond the narrow focus on production and profit that drives negative side effects. It is possible that reflexivity could go beyond technical solutions and include changing social structures that have become problematic and high risk. Romano (2012) argues that reflexive modernization does not necessarily support maintaining the current system, dominated by the economic growth imperative. In light of the environmental crisis we now face, reflexivity may be more in line with the logic of degrowth: the purposeful contraction of production and consumption in wealthy countries to stay within biophysical limits (Kallis 2018). Thus, if overproduction and overconsumption are increasing environmental risks, pushing us toward ecological collapse, then reprioritizing and restructuring society away from growth, to better support social and ecological well-being, would be a reflexive response. This would be a clear example of societal-level "self-confrontation."

However, we also see anti-reflexivity forces that aim to stymie and stop reflexive policies, even those that represent minor reforms to reduce risks. McCright and Dunlap (2010) discuss how the fossil fuel industry and conservative groups have worked to hinder reflexivity in terms of responding to climate change. In addition, Cordner's (2016) work illustrates how the chemical industry actively worked to block the regulation of toxic flame retardants. While we may see reflexivity in terms of scientific findings, concerned citizens, advocacy groups, and social movements, we also see powerful actors working to stop reflexivity in its tracks. These actors invest significant resources in an attempt to maintain the status quo. As argued by Boström and colleagues (2017: 13), it is "crucial to address the powerful forces that deliberately and strategically counteract reflexivity, which many times are the same forces that create environmental destruction." Compared to the US, there are more environmental protections in place in the European Union that are in-line with reflexive modernization. For example, the REACH program for regulating chemicals and cap and trade programs to reduce greenhouse gas emissions. In the US context, we find more cases where anti-reflexivity forces have successfully blocked reflexive policy, even incremental reforms.

In terms of reflexivity as a societal solution to address our environmental crisis, we see that reflexivity alone is not enough. Climate change is a prime example. Despite reflexive scientists and citizens and the rise of a global climate movement, we do not see the policies and programs necessary to address the problem. In this case, reflexivity does tell us more about what society ought to be doing than what it necessarily is doing (Boström et al. 2017). Perhaps reflexivity cannot be fully realized because the current system undermines the potential to be reflexive. Even if scientists, citizens, and social movements are reflexive, power asymmetries and neoliberal ideology continue to stymie reflexivity at the top levels of governance and decision-making. How can we shift priorities to address our environmental crisis in a system that continues to be controlled by those that benefit from the status quo?

Ecological Modernization

Ecological modernization theory (EMT) also emerged from European scholars and entails a more defined solution pathway for exactly how society should modernize to address environmental impacts. EMT posits that society can reduce environmental impacts through the use of science, technology, markets, and policy reforms and specifically supports the position that we can support economic growth while addressing environmental impacts (Mol and Spaargaren 2000, Mol et al. 2013). Economic growth is considered a constant, an assumed condition of the global economy that is positive in general. Thus, EM involves simultaneously reducing environmental risks and increasing economic growth, or "green growth." The task remains finding the right technologies and making the right adjustments to the capitalist system to effectively address environmental impacts. In contrast to reflexive modernization, EM involves more top-down, state-led action rather than bottom-up action led by citizens and social movements (Fisher and Jorgenson 2019).

According to EMT, while development and economic growth do indeed result in negative environmental impacts, these impacts will diminish as growth continues and as technology, economic resources, markets, and policies are used to create effective solutions (Mol and Spaargaren 2000, Mol et al. 2013). While economic growth might result in negative environmental impacts in the early stages of economic development, technological innovation and reforms can "decouple" environmental impacts and economic growth as development continues. Therefore, economic growth can continue while environmental impacts are reduced. The Environmental Kuznet's curve describes this relationship: environmental impacts increase with development to a point and then decrease with further economic development. Thus, impacts are both caused and then later addressed through economic development when an "environmental rationality" becomes central in the process of modernization (Sapinski 2017).

According to EMT, addressing environmental impacts is not only compatible with growth but is aided by economic growth through "green growth." It is a "greening" of the system that largely maintains the same priorities and structures. This is indeed an optimistic vision (Fisher and Jorgenson 2019), and is again supported by more examples from Europe than other regions. Specific examples of EM have been found in the actions of individual firms that "go green" as well as specific policy reforms, market incentives, and green stimulus programs. In terms of climate change, carbon markets represent an attempt to tweak the market to reduce emissions, yet with slow and limited results (Stuart et al. 2019). However, it may be that results are not the focus of some EMT scholars, who remain more focused on the narrative of EMT and how "environmental rationality" emerges as a social phenomenon (Mol et al. 2013). The danger lies in relying on a solution pathway that may be unable to address our escalating existential threats. In this case, the EM narrative would represent a myth, a myth that is appealing and draws attention and resources away from other solution pathways (Sapinski 2017).

EMT relies heavily on faith in new technologies to reduce environmental impacts. Technological optimism refers to an overall faith in the ability of technology to solve environmental problems. York and Clark (2010: 481) describe technological optimism in detail as it relates to EMT: "technological breakthroughs will serve as the means to address each and every environmental problem that arises, allowing society to overcome natural limits and all socio-ecological challenges." Techno-optimists believe that it is not necessary to challenge the current political-economic social order because we can use science and technology to overcome environmental problems. This prescription indicates that environmental problems are viewed primarily as technical problems that we can engineer solutions to. This is especially clear in the case of geoengineering as a techno-fix to address climate change. This could involve reflecting solar radiation back into space or sucking carbon dioxide out of the atmosphere. In both cases, the technology is nowhere near ready for widespread, safe, or effective use, yet the ideas are gaining support, most likely because they do not challenge a fossil fuel-based and growth-driven system (Gunderson et al. 2018, Stuart et al. 2019). In addition, while extensive resources have been invested in energy efficiency and renewable energy technologies, increasing evidence reveals the limitation of these technological fixes within a growing economy.

Environmental sociologists have discovered paradoxical outcomes that bring into question the assumption that technology can or will reduce environmental impacts. Studies have found evidence in accord with the Jevons paradox, named after the economist William Stanley Jevons, who discovered that higher efficiency in steam engines increased total coal consumption (Clark and Foster 2001). Other studies have found additional associations between increased resource use despite improved efficiency (e.g., York 2010, Clement 2011, York et al. 2011, York and McGee 2016). This is paradoxical because it is largely assumed that improvements in efficiency will result in a decrease in total resource use, yet there is an association between efficiency and increased impacts due to increases in consumption (York and McGee 2016). This phenomenon is also referred to as the "rebound effect," or when the benefits of efficiency gains are partially or fully offset by increases in total resource use (Santarius 2012). While causation is difficult to prove, it is likely that improvements in efficiency reduce prices per economic unit, which increases the use of the given resource or investment in the use of other resources (see Santarius, 2012; York and McGee 2016). In summary, efficiency gains are in many cases failing to result in lower total impacts due to overall increases in production and consumption. However, in a reduced or steady state of consumption, efficiency could result in lower impacts.

It is also largely believed that the growth of alternative energy sources will result in the replacement and phasing out of coal and other fossil fuels; however, this is not what environmental sociologists have found. Illustrating another paradoxical relationship, increases in renewable sources of energy have not been fully displacing existing energy sources. This adds up to an increase in total energy use and not the reduction in carbon emissions that renewable energy sources could provide. This was clearly documented by York (2012b) and York and Bell (2019) who illustrate how renewables are only minimally displacing fossil fuels and that in general they are being used *in addition* to fossil fuels, with an increase in total energy use. Renewable sources also have a lower energy return on energy invested (EROEI), meaning that they will not supply the same rates of energy as existing fossil fuel sources (e.g., 60:1 for coal compared to 18:1 for wind and 6:1 for solar) (Hall et al. 2014). Therefore, for renewables to result in a total decrease in carbon emissions, we must not only replace fossil fuel sources but also reduce total energy consumption—which continues to go up.

Public Sociology: The Renewable Energy "Transition"

Richard York and colleagues have made substantial contributions toward our understanding of climate change solutions through revealing that the energy "transition" is not much of a transition in terms of moving away from fossil fuels and using renewable energy sources instead. York's (2012b) findings published in *Nature Climate Change* illustrate how growth in non-fossil fuel energy has only a very modest effect on reducing the use of fossil fuels, with between four and thirteen units of non-fossil energy used to displace one unit of fossil energy (York 2012b). This work received widespread media attention, including on the British Broadcasting Corporation (BBC) News.

Richard York and Shannon Bell (2019) further illustrate this alarming trend. They explain how data about the energy transition focuses on statistics and figures that obscure the fact that fossil fuel sources are not being reduced at a rate anywhere near what is necessary to stay within global targets. The authors explain:

> We should not assume that growth in the production of renewable energy sources is indicative of a move away from fossil fuels. Indeed, if the current moment of change in energy composition is like previous ones, we may expect simply an expansion of the overall amount of energy that is produced.

This work has significant implications in terms of climate change policy. Many people are shocked and surprised to learn that renewable energy is not displacing fossil fuel sources as expected. In a system with increasing total energy use, adding renewable sources has not reduced carbon emissions. As York (2017: 1) also reveals upon analyzing why petroleum did not save the whales, there is "limited potential for technological developments to help overcome environmental problems without concurrent political, economic, and social change." It is not enough to simply replace one technology with another. We also need to design pathways specifically aimed at addressing environmental impacts. In addition to increasing renewable sources, we must also actively reduce the use of fossil fuels and limit increases in total energy use. In terms of policy, this means that in addition to increasing alternative energy we need to reduce fossil fuel use directly. This could involve a carbon tax and dividend program (Schor 2015) or nationalizing and subsequently phasing out the fossil fuel industry (Gunderson 2019).

Despite these paradoxical relationships, do we still find signs of globally reduced environmental impacts with increasing levels of economic growth? Studies have explored if we see empirical evidence of the decoupling of economic growth from environmental harm, as suggested by EMT. To reduce environmental impacts, this decoupling would have to be *absolute*, meaning that overall impacts are lower, not just the impacts per unit of production (*relative* decoupling). Studies report mixed findings, depending on the scale and location of analysis. While trends in accord with EMT have been found in some European cases, other case studies show that environmental impacts continue to increase with economic growth (contradicting what we would expect, according to the Environmental Kuznet's Curve) or that impacts reduced in one place emerge in another (e.g., York et al. 2003a,b; Longo and York 2008). The Kuznet's Curve may describe a trend that is dependent on region and context, and on which environmental harm is being analyzed. In many cases, examples of EM in the Global North may result in increasing environmental impacts in the Global South—or impact displacement (Givens et al. 2019). Jorgenson (2016) presents the results of a number of global-scale empirical studies that do not support predictions in line with EMT. In summary, empirical evidence has raised substantial doubts about EMT as a viable solution pathway for global environmental threats.

A critical question is whether carbon emissions can be decoupled from economic growth. Jorgenson and Clark (2012) used models and statistical analyses to demonstrate a strong relationship between GDP per capita and carbon emissions in developed nations, consistent over time. Knight and Schor (2012) found no evidence for absolute decoupling between carbon emissions and GDP between 1991 and 2008. At a national level, they found cases of modest relative decoupling in developed nations that was largely a result of increased carbon-intensive production in developing nations, yet once trade-related emissions were included almost no countries showed signs of absolute decoupling (Knight and Schor 2014). Schor and Jorgenson (2019) present a thorough synthesis of findings, illustrating how GDP and carbon emissions are indeed still very coupled and, while there are some cases where you can see relative decoupling, there is no evidence to support that the absolute decoupling necessary to achieve emissions targets can occur. They quote climate scientist Kevin Anderson who stated: "Put bluntly, climate change commitments are incompatible with short- to medium-term economic growth." Anderson has also criticized the standard climate models that depend on negative emissions technologies to stay within global targets, emphasizing how relying on unproven technologies is a risky and dangerous gamble. If we lack evidence that technology can sustain GDP growth while keeping global temperatures within safe targets, at what point does a reliance on "green growth" become a moral hazard?

Beyond environmental sociology, other scholars also argue that there is no convincing evidence for the absolute decoupling of material resources and that if there is evidence for modest decoupling of carbon, we do not see this decoupling occurring *at a rate fast enough* to prevent warming over 2°C (Hickel and Kallis 2019, Parrique et al. 2019). In other words, it may not be a matter of whether absolute decoupling of carbon emissions is possible, but if it is possible at a rate fast enough to prevent catastrophic climate impacts. As we witness increases in human suffering and loss, there are important questions to consider. Can we rely on EM and techno-fixes despite a lack of evidence that they will be reliable? By focusing on EM are there other possibilities that we are not considering that might be more effective and less risky? Based on the empirical research, critical scholars continue to argue that "green growth" will be unable to address climate change and is highly risky. Why then is it so heavily promoted? Why does it remain the dominant narrative influencing both climate modeling scenarios and global climate policy? Gunderson and colleagues (2018) argue that a focus on "green growth" as the solution to climate change represents strategic ideology used to conceal the underlying contradiction between climate stability and a growth-dependent capitalist system. This ideology continues to protect vested interests who benefit from the status quo: a fossil fuel-based and growth-oriented society. Grunwald (2018) explains that, based on the evidence, an EM approach is not only very risky but also immoral. We cannot predict the technologies and innovations of the future, but can we assume there will be discoveries that result in the absolute decoupling necessary to keep global warming within 2°C? Due to the risk, this is a moral gamble, and a very high-stakes gamble, as life as we know it is on the line. Grunwald (2018: 1854, 1860) argues that the EM approach to the environmental crisis is "morally hazardous because it expects to overcome the ecological crisis by technological progress and its acceleration only, ignoring the ambivalences of technology and the issue of unintended side effects." It is "the position of a moral gambler who bets everything on one horse." Given what is at stake, is the EM gamble worth the risk? And by focusing on optimistic and appealing EM solutions, are we overlooking other options that could more quickly and justly minimize escalating environmental threats?

Structural Changes

In this section, the work of Schor and Jorgenson (2019: 322) will guide our analysis of structural change. They ask critically important questions about the climate crisis with vast societal implications: "Can the magnitude of required emissions reductions be achieved while leaving the basic structures of the economy unchanged? Or does the scale of the challenge facing us require more systemic change?" This discussion largely focuses on affluent countries, whose overproduction and overconsumption have contributed the most carbon emissions.

First, we need to understand what people mean when they talk about structural or systemic change. These changes go beyond technologies, market-based solutions, or minor tweaks to our current political economy, and instead reshape the system. It is difficult to say at what point a change reshapes the system. Some cases might be obvious, yet others may represent smaller but important steps that lead to a series of systemic changes. Andre Gorz (1968) discusses the importance of "non-reformist reforms" that shift the realm of what is possible and open up pathways for more transformational changes. Instead of focusing first on theories and visions of new systems (often associated with widely misunderstood terms), here we are going to first examine proposals for specific structural changes that are supported by empirical evidence. We will then see how these structural changes align with different visions of a new system and discuss possible synergies for most effectively and justly addressing our environmental crisis.

To center this discussion, we will continue to focus primarily on structural changes to address the climate crisis, yet these same changes would also help alleviate the drivers of biodiversity loss, pollution, and other environmental impacts. When Schor and Jorgenson (2019: 322) talk about systemic or structural changes to address the climate crisis, they mean "changes in the operation of the economy that both reduce emissions and yield a range of other benefits." They propose a few specific strategies that, based on empirical evidence, are likely to be effective at reducing carbon emissions and would also alleviate other social problems, some seemingly unrelated to the environment. Two structural changes they propose are work time reduction and a reduction in the concentration of wealth.

Work time reduction (WTR) is being proposed not only by environmental sociologists but also by ecological economists and a range of other scientists. WTR would involve reducing annual working hours to a new standard, without decreases in pay or loss of benefits, and would likely also involve models for work sharing. Work sharing allows for less hours worked while avoiding unemployment (Schor 2015). There are multiple ways to approach WTR, including increasing holidays each year, limiting the number of working hours per week, increasing sick leave and maternity and paternity leave, and offering pre-retirement transitions (Pullinger 2014). Examples of WTR already exist. Some have been temporary policies during economic downturns and most cases have been in the European Union. There are both environmental and social benefits associated with WTR.

Studies indicate that WTR can reduce carbon emissions and ecological footprints (Knight et al. 2013, Schor and Jorgenson 2019). Shorter working hours involve lower rates of production and reduce resources and energy use. Working hours are associated with energy consumption (Fitzgerald et al. 2015), and by some estimates if working hours were reduced, instead of using productivity gains for increased production, the US would consume 20 percent less energy (Rosnick and Weisbrot 2006). Another estimate indicates that if we reduce working hours 0.5 percent annually over the next century we can "eliminate about one-quarter to one-half, if not more, of any warming that is not already locked in" (Rosnick 2013: 124). In general, because longer working hours are associated with increased carbon emissions, ecological footprints, and energy use, WTR represents a potentially powerful mitigation strategy (Schor and Jorgenson 2019). WTR does not necessarily guarantee less environmental impacts, because leisure could be spent doing environmentally harmful activities such as shopping or travel (Knight et al. 2013, Gunderson 2019). Therefore, other changes, such as reduced advertising (described below), would also be important to encourage low-impact activities.

In terms of social benefits, WTR could help to increase levels of employment, improve quality of life, and enhance overall well-being. In 1930, as productivity levels were rapidly increasing, John Maynard Keynes predicted that by 2030 people would only work 15 hours each week to support their material needs. However, instead, these productivity gains have been used to increase production per person. Many workers continue to do unfulfilling and alienating work without enough time for family, hobbies, creativity, and general human flourishing. In Europe, where working time is around 35 hours a week, labor unions have recently demanded WTR (Harper 2017, Bulman 2018). If a renewed labor movement and the environmental movement both demanded WTR, they could represent a powerful force for change and help address the false antagonism between jobs and the environment (see Gunderson 2019).

While incorporating WTR and work-sharing could increase social and environmental benefits, policies at the federal level would be needed to standardize WTR and to allow for the full range of social and environmental benefits. For example, in the current US system where benefits are tied to a 40-hour work week, we cannot expect a widespread voluntary transition to reduced working hours. It would require government support. It would indeed represent a significant structural change if everyone worked no more than 20 hours a week and everyone had full access to health care and other benefits. WTR could surely help to slow down over-production, but other changes would be necessary.

Schor and Jorgenson (2019) also call for structural changes to address the staggering levels of economic inequality. While seemingly unrelated, economic inequality is positively associated with carbon emissions (Schor 2015, Jorgenson et al. 2016a and 2017, Knight et al. 2017). We have already examined how the very rich have the greatest impacts, including carbon emissions. Addressing inequality through the redistribution of wealth would likely be an effective mitigation strategy. Therefore, a wealth tax, income cap, or other redistributive measure could reduce the overconsumption of unnecessary resources. A carbon tax with a dividend that is paid to lower income groups would be a way to reduce carbon emissions and redistribute wealth (Schor and Jorgenson 2019). In addition, other tax reforms could discourage the consumption of unnecessary or luxury goods. Taxes could be placed on items such as the additional square footage of large homes, private planes and boats, and the carbon emissions associated with goods, services, and transportation. Such measures could help reduce carbon emissions and address other social issues, as economic inequality remains damaging to society in general, with negative impacts to health and well-being (Hill and Jorgenson 2018).

Schor and Jorgenson (2019), among many others, also call for the abandonment of GDP as an indicator of social progress. As discussed earlier in this chapter, prioritizing GDP growth is being increasingly deemed problematic— steering us toward ever increasing levels of production at the expense of social and ecological well-being. In terms of climate change, Schor and Jorgenson (2019: 322) state that we must "abandon the growth-at-all-costs mentality that has dominated policy-making and focus on additional emissions-reducing policies." This alone would likely not address our environmental crisis; however, prioritizing indicators of well-being instead of GDP would make WTR and addressing inequality more possible. In other words, while not necessarily a significant structural change, using social indicators prioritizing well-being rather than growth is a complementary strategy that can allow for structural change.

Another complementary strategy is to restrict the advertising that drives citizens to become super-consumers. Advertising continues to create desires that fuel consumption. Advertising restrictions could be used to reduce the overconsumption of unnecessary goods, or "false needs" created through manipulation (Marcuse 1964). As discussed in the previous chapter, advertising influences individuals' views of themselves and their social status. It compels them to buy unnecessary products to address manufactured dissatisfaction. While restricting advertising may seem "un-American," even in the US advertisements aimed at children were banned until 1984 (Molotsky 1988). Banning advertising for luxury, harmful, or status commodities could significantly help reduce overconsumption, as well as banning advertising in public spaces and directed at children. Advertising restrictions complement WTR and wealth redistribution. In particular, reduced advertising would help ensure that increased free time due to WTR did not result in increased levels of consumption.

While there are certainly other ideas about structural changes, these examples provide an idea of what these strategies could entail—and in *all* cases there would be immense challenges due to current power relations. As depicted long ago by both Marx and Gramsci, throughout human history those in power attempt to retain power. This has been called "social reproduction" (Wright 2010) as well as "anti-reflexivity" (McCright and Dunlap 2010). The work of Klein (2015) and Brulle (2018a,b), among many others, illustrates how our current political system is rigid and unchanging in order to protect the individuals and corporations who benefit most from a growth-oriented, fossil fuel-based society. This is one reason the US has been demoted to the status of a "flawed democracy" (Economist Intelligence Unit 2019). The current US government is not representing the views of its citizens, who polls show largely support immediate climate action. Thus, structural changes of any sort would first require a shift in power—away from those prioritizing economic growth for the few and toward those who want to prioritize climate stability, biodiversity, equality, and social well-being. This shift involves challenging neoliberal ideology that continues to make collective efforts to address environmental impacts or help people seem like threatening interference. Effectively addressing our environmental crisis also requires confronting the ideology of "green growth" and collectively deciding what risks we are willing to take moving forward.

One can imagine a world where these power relations have shifted and democracy is restored to a point where world governments all took bold action to protect citizens from environmental threats. For example, to most quickly and effectively curb fossil fuel use, governments could implement a carbon tax and dividend program, and could also buy out or nationalize fossil fuel companies to phase out fossil fuels in a controlled way (while *replacing* them with renewable energy sources). Governments could also focus on the biggest polluters, who disproportionately contribute to carbon emissions (Jorgenson et al. 2016b). Yet, this requires bold and strong government action, something in opposition to neoliberal ideology and in opposition to the interests of those who benefit most from the current system. In other words, structural changes are not impossible, yet as we will examine in the next chapter, they would likely require a forceful social movement that challenges power and demands change.

Public Sociology: Targeting Super-Polluters

What if we could target a few major sources of pollution and significantly reduce overall emissions? This would be getting the biggest "bang for your buck" in terms of solution strategies. Environmental sociologist William Freudenburg proposed strategies years ago that focus on "disproportionality." In other words, some firms (or individuals) pollute much more than others; therefore, an efficient solution strategy is to target the biggest polluters for emissions reductions. These ideas have continued to inform work in environmental sociology.

In an article titled, "This could be a completely different strategy for tackling the world's carbon emissions," (Harvey 2016) Andrew Jorgenson, Wesley Longhofer, and Don Grant's work on disproportionality and power plants (2016b) was highlighted in *The Washington Post* along with commentary from Thomas Dietz on the implications of their findings. The article states that a "1 percent increase in disproportionality leads to a 0.37 percent increase in overall national-level carbon emissions from fossil fuel power plants." Jorgenson explained to the reporter, "it means that tackling just the few, biggest carbon emitters among a nation's power plants—which are typically those contributing to the inequalities in power plant emissions on a national level—can be an effective climate change mitigation strategy." Dietz told the Post, "instead of targeting all power plants in a country, one could get big reductions with relatively less cost by targeting the most inefficient plants." This work can inform strategies to efficiently and quickly reduce emissions through focusing on high-emitting targets (Harvey 2016).

Mary Collins' research has also illustrated the importance of addressing super-polluters in terms of carbon emissions and toxic chemical pollution. Collins and Anya Galli Robertson (2019) illustrate how focusing on super-polluters could be a very effective approach to reduce carbon emissions. Collins et al.'s previous work (2016) revealed the existence of "toxic outliers" as an environmental justice issue. Collins and others (2020) used EPA data and examined toxic releases in over 300 industries, finding cases of super-polluters in a wide range of sectors. In some cases, just a few facilities in a sector were responsible for half of all industry emissions. These findings have important implications for identifying effective solutions to address pollution, mitigate climate change, and protect communities.

While targeting super-polluters may not represent a structural change, adopting such an approach could represent an effective step as well as a signal of shifting political alliances that could open up pathways for bigger changes. While powerful firms have lobbied and fought against regulations and pollution control, public pressure and a growing climate movement could pressure policymakers to prioritize their constituents over corporate interests. In some cases, politicians who have refused to change their alliances and better protect their constituents have been replaced by new representatives with different priorities.

Toward a New System?

When people say "system change" what do they mean? They may mean adopting some of the strategies for structural change discussed above. In addition, some people may have a specific "new system" in mind, such as a system based on socialism or degrowth. Indeed, if all of the structural changes described above were adopted in a country like the US, it would surely result in something many of us would see as a "new system." Would this system be capitalist? Would it be socialist? Would it be an eco-socialist or degrowth society? Because these terms are so widely misused, some people prefer to discuss specific strategies like the ones described above while avoiding terms that might conjure up confusion. While the use of terms such as *socialism* and *capitalism* surely lead to misunderstandings, rather than ignore them we will define them in ways that focus on how to best address environmental impacts and support ecological and social well-being.

First, how do we define capitalism? Some people say that capitalism is an economic system where there is private property, markets to distribute goods, and money used as a basis of exchange. However, others define capitalism as an economic system with specific class and ownership relations benefiting the wealthy few, and as a system that continually accumulates wealth and continues to expand for the sake of more wealth accumulation. In other words, capitalism is growth-dependent and must always expand due to the forces at play (the ToP). While people certainly speak about capitalism in different ways with different ideas in mind, there is agreement among many scholars that growth dependency and ever-expanding production and profits are *the* defining features of capitalism. This definition suggests that a capitalist system will by definition always grow.

Why must a capitalist system always grow? The explanation behind this growth is that in a capitalist system with the goal of maximizing profits, surplus must be reinvested to increase production and future profits. This increases both production and the advertising necessary to sell products, whether or not they increase well-being or cause environmental damage. Firms in many cases must adhere to this model due to the realities of debt, competition, and investment. "Get big or get out" is the norm in many sectors. In order to maximize profits, this system also incentivizes cost-cutting, the externalization of environmental damage, and paying workers low wages. Even a business owner who cares about the environment and workers faces significant challenges prioritizing these concerns while staying competitive in a capitalist system. This is not to say that the system could not be improved. If governments required lower pollution or higher wages, then all firms would need to adapt to the new rules or be penalized. Yet, in many cases the power of firms influences government, ensuring that environmental laws do not overly impact profit. According to this definition, it is the ToP of the capitalist system that both drives our environmental crisis and also prevents solutions from being effective.

What about socialism as a new system? The idea of socialism emerged as an alternative to capitalism in response to the injustices related to worker exploitation and class power witnessed by Marx during the industrial revolution. His vision of socialism included worker control over the means of production, equality, and prioritizing the well-being of all people. However, countries that have attempted to adopt a "socialist" model have largely resulted in authoritarian governments who prioritized economic growth at the expense of social justice and environmental protection. These are cases of what Erik Olin Wright (2010) calls "statism," not socialism, because the means of production were owned almost exclusively by the state and these models lacked democracy, worker control of production, and the prioritization of well-being. In other words, the "actually existing" examples of "socialism" do not match the socialist vision and were in many ways simply state-operated capitalist systems.

Democratic socialism emphasizes what was lacking in the cases of statism, and entails prioritizing equality and well-being, democratization of work, and representation through democratic processes. It is a form of socialism that leaves room for society to decide if economic growth should be prioritized. As explained by Kallis (2019: 267): "Capitalism is geared to grow or die. Socialism could, at least in principle, secure a better quality of life with less resources and energy, and distribute them more equally." If we believe that capitalism inherently involves perpetual economic growth, then a true alternative to capitalism would also need to cast off the growth imperative. Marcuse (1967: 3) also explains that "even Marx was still too tied to the notion of a continuum of progress, that even his idea of socialism may not yet represent, or no longer represent, the determinate negation of capitalism it was supposed to." Thus, if socialism is a true negation of capitalism, it would need to take a position against the notion of never-ending economic growth.

Degrowth specifically confronts the economic growth imperative, presenting a vision of societies living well within ecological limits. As an alternative economic system to address our environmental crisis, degrowth acknowledges that economic growth is at odds with ecological sustainability and calls for a retraction in material and energy use in wealthy countries, to exist within biophysical limits (Kallis 2018). Visions of a degrowth society include many of the strategies already mentioned here: WTR, restricting advertising, redistributing wealth, and other ways to improve ecological and social well-being. Degrowth is described as working less, buying less, sharing more, and living more simply in a way that could make people happier and improve quality of life. Rather than a sacrifice, it is framed as an opportunity to improve social well-being. Environmental sociologists have identified degrowth as a vision worth exploring further (Gunderson et al. 2018, Schor and Jorgenson 2019).

Finally, eco-socialism represents an extension of democratic socialism focused on staying within biophysical limits. In many ways it complements degrowth. Eco-socialists emphasize addressing environmental impacts and ecological sustainability in addition to the socialist goals of equality, democracy, and well-being. Löwy (2006) describes eco-socialism as "putting human and planetary needs first and foremost." Foster (2013: 16) describes key elements of eco-socialism to include: "(1) social use, not ownership, of nature; (2) rational regulation by the associated producers of the metabolic relation between humanity and nature; and (3) satisfaction of communal needs—not only of present but also future generations (and life itself)." Baer (2019) specifically describes "democratic eco-socialism" as recognizing that we live on a finite planet with ecological limits and rejecting the prioritization of economic growth in order to protect future generations. Many eco-socialists would likely support the strategies for structural change described here, and likely other changes including democratizing the workplace and worker ownership of production—which are also supported by many degrowthers (Kallis 2018).

What aligns eco-socialism and degrowth as complementary visions is the concept of subordinating economic goals to social and ecological well-being. Both Karl Polanyi's and Ulrich Beck's works also support this concept. Polanyi (1944) focuses on the concept of *embeddedness* and how the economic system should be embedded within the social system, rather than dominating the social order. Polanyi argues that the economies of earlier societies functioned based on systems of reciprocity and social welfare rather than as a market of commodities for the pursuit of profit maximization. Polanyi thus calls for a shift in priorities that protect people and nature. Beck (1992) also alludes to a need to shift priorities away from production and profit maximization to better address environmental risks. Being reflexive could very well entail a systemic transformation, in which we prioritize social and ecological well-being, subordinating economic goals to social goals in order to protect ourselves from existential threats. These notions are also increasingly supported by climate activists, as many hold signs demanding that world leaders "Put People Before Profit." Some people dismiss these ideas as utopian and state that they are "never going to happen," yet others argue that these visions are critical to have a clear direction to work towards.

We Cannot Be Radical Enough

This chapter is the longest in the book because, as we face escalating existential threats, it is critical that we identify the most effective and just solutions and act to push them forward. As our environmental crisis impacts us more each day, many people feel paralyzed by existential dread and fall into despair or denial. Yet solutions have already been identified, studied, and designed. Many of these solutions complement each other and could be pursued simultaneously. The visions for a new system we explored are in many ways utopian, but not impossible. In fact, we can see how, through implementing the strategies for structural change outlined, we could get very close to some of these utopian visions.

How quickly we identify and implement solutions matters. Facing existential threats, we need to quickly implement solutions that are the most effective and just in order to avoid outcomes that scientists state would be catastrophic. Time is limited and running out. Therefore, the solutions that we could have implemented a decade or two ago now may not be enough. Solutions to support the most sustainable and just future, with the minimal global changes, will now have to be bold, radical, and transformative. The 2018 IPCC special report summary specifically calls for "rapid, far-reaching, and unprecedented changes in all aspects of society." The famous naturalist David Attenborough stated that when it comes to climate change, "we cannot be radical enough." In other words, if we choose bold and transformative solutions we may be able to minimize suffering and loss and steer ourselves on a path toward the most sustainable and just possible future.

A major challenge remains: many people fail to see that structural changes or another social order with better social and ecological outcomes are even possible. The ideologies of today keep telling us that the way things are now is the only way, there are no alternatives, and we can only make minor tweaks to the current system. However, the current system has only been in place a few hundred years, which is a very short time in the span of human existence. More and more people are realizing that bigger changes are possible. The surge in support for Democratic Socialist political candidates, polls showing increased support for "socialist" ideas to protect well-being, and support to put the environment before the economy indicate that these types of changes are increasingly possible. But they will require not only raising awareness but unprecedented mobilization to challenge existing powers and demand change.

Discussion Questions

1. How would abandoning GDP growth as a social priority open up opportunities to address environmental impacts and our escalating environmental crises?
2. What are some of the contributions and limitations of individual-focused solutions?
3. What types of impacts can consumers try to avoid? What allows or limits this avoidance?
4. What do the two modernization theories presented in this chapter have in common and how are they different? Do you think we see these types of modernization occurring?
5. What structural changes do you think are most important to implement? Why?

6. Compare the "new systems" described in the chapter. What aspects do you find appealing, if any, related to each of the new system "visions" presented?

Suggested Reading

Boström, M., R. Lidskog, & Y. Uggla. (2017). A reflexive look at reflexivity in environmental sociology. *Environmental Sociology* 3(1): 6–16.

Foster, J. B. (2020). "Why ecological revolution?" In *Environmental Sociology: From Analysis to Action*. Edited by L. King and D. M. Auriffeille. Lanham, MD: Rowman & Littlefield.

Jorgenson, A., W. Longhofer, & D. Grant. (2016). Disproportionality in power plants' carbon emissions: a cross-national study. *Scientific Reports* 6: 28661.

Knight, K., E. Rosa, & J. Schor. (2013). Could working less reduce pressures on the environment?: A cross-national panel analysis of OECD countries, 1970–2007. *Global Environmental Change* 23: 691–700.

Lorenzen, J. A. (2014). Green consumption and social change: debates over responsibility, private action, and access. *Sociology Compass* 8(8): 1063–1081.

McCright, A. M., & R. E. Dunlap. (2010). Anti-reflexivity. *Theory, Culture & Society* 27(2–3): 100–133.

MacKendrick, N., & L. M. Stevens. (2016). Taking back a little bit of control: Managing the contaminated body through consumption. *Sociological Forum* 31(2): 310–329.

Schor, J. B., & A. K. Jorgenson. (2019). Is it too late for growth? *Review of Radical Political Economics* 51(2): 320–329.

Stuart, D., R. Gunderson, & B. Petersen. (2020). *Climate Change Solutions: Beyond the Capital-Climate Contradiction*. Ann Arbor: University of Michigan Press.

York, R., & S. E. Bell. (2019). Energy transitions or additions? Why a transition from fossil fuels requires more than the growth of renewable energy. *Energy Research & Social Science* 51: 40–43.

5
Moving Forward

While a number of solutions were discussed in the previous chapter, the critical question remains: how do we get there? Whatever solutions are likely to be the most effective and just must not only be identified but pushed forward. Thus, understanding social movements and how social change happens is critically important. This chapter concludes the book by examining the role of social movements and pathways for social change as well as discussing what will likely be critical topics and questions for environmental sociologists to examine moving forward. We will inevitably experience an increasingly altered planet and it will be important to understand how these alterations impact humans, both physically and emotionally, as well as how people can adapt, come together, and create resilient communities. At the same time, it will be important to further examine challenges to the status quo and the power struggles that emerge as solutions to the climate and biodiversity crises are put forward.

While it is easy to feel discouraged by the challenges ahead and the magnitude of what is at stake, it is important to remain honest about these realities. Rather than letting the truth lead to paralysis or fatalism, we can harness the truth to push forward the most effective and just solutions. It is nowhere near "too late" to reduce the impacts of our environmental crisis, as there are so many ways we can still work to protect and improve social and ecological well-being.

There will also be increasing opportunities for environmental sociologists and other scholars to examine the ever-changing relationships between humans and the biophysical world. A changing environment, even in a state of crisis, also creates opportunities to understand how humans can come together, help each other, and create resilient communities in the face of hardship.

Social Movements and Social Change

Environmental sociologists widely agree that whether solutions come in the form of policy reforms or radical economic and social transformation, social movements play a key role in pushing solutions forward. Scholars have studied environmental social movements for decades and examined the US environmental movement (e.g., Brulle 2000), movements in the Global South (e.g., Lewis 2009), as well as environmental health movements (e.g., McCormick et al. 2003, Cordner and Brown 2015), environmental justice movements (e.g., Bullard and Johnson 2000, Harrison 2016), indigenous environmental movements (e.g., Clark 2002), and energy transition movements (e.g., Kallman and Frickel 2019). Environmental sociologists examine the discourse and framing of social movements as well as movement histories, strategies, resources, and participants. Social movements have been integral in pushing forward important environmental legislation and in protecting ecosystems and communities. Due to the pressing nature of the existential threats we face, here we focus on what social movements mean in terms of pushing forward the necessary changes to address these threats and also how these changes could happen based on theories of social transformation.

First, what is a social movement? People define social movements in different ways, yet some characteristics are common across definitions. According to many scholars (e.g., Smelser 1962, Tilly 1978, McAdam 2017), social movements consist of people with a shared concern, belief, or common purpose. They represent an organized effort in which people actively mobilize to change society in the face of opposition.

Social movements also use specific tactics and forms of agitation when windows of social and political opportunity open. Many movements emerge in response to social deprivation or strain that is not being addressed adequately by government. Individuals may unite behind similar beliefs regarding the causes of and solutions to deprivation and strain, forming a collective identity. Finally, social movements consist of informal networks and can include heterogeneous organizations and actors, either because origins are diverse or because of ruptures leading to distinctive strands within a movement.

Despite divergent definitions regarding what constitutes a social movement, scholars agree that social movements are key drivers of social change. Movements may aim to change individual behaviors or to reform or transform an entire system. Prominent examples of system-focused social movements include the Civil Rights Movement, the Women's Suffrage Movement, and movements attempting to change political leadership or gain independence from outside rule. Some movements succeed when new rights or forms of access are granted to previously excluded groups, while other movements demand systemic changes. A transformative movement, compared to reformative movement, seeks to change the system as a whole. According to prominent social movement theorists, revolutionary outcomes occur when people "begin to redefine the fundamental values of the entire system in which they find themselves" (Smelser 1962) and one set of powers is replaced by another (Tilly 1978).

Social movements emerge, either succeed or fail, and then usually dissolve. A key question in social movement analysis remains: Under what conditions do social movements succeed? The answer to this question is not simple and continues to be widely debated. Commonly cited determinants of social movement success include the extent of the strain experienced by the population, the growth and extent of a shared belief and identity, events that trigger large responses, the ability to create a compelling narrative that frames an issue as moral and elicits emotional responses, the resources available to the groups involved, political openings or barriers, the capacity to be disruptive, the population involved in mobilization, whether mobilizations are allowed or suppressed, and the overall power of the opposition (Smelser 1962, Tilly 1978, Chenoweth and Stephan 2011, Tufekci 2017, Wright 2019). Based on all of these factors, it is difficult to identify what will make a specific social movement successful, but we do know that social movements remain a key component of social change.

How does social change happen? Social change is largely unpredictable, but we can draw insights from a few different theories based on historical analyses. While there are many theories of social change, we explore two here. First, Karl Polanyi's book *The Great Transformation* (1944) describes examples of social change to address social deprivation and strain during several different time periods. Brechin and Fenner (2017) revisit Polanyi's ideas about social transformation and its relevance for environmental sociology. Polanyi describes a pattern in society where the expansion of markets and the attempted commodification of false commodities (land, labor, and money) result in harms that trigger societal responses. Polanyi's pattern is as follows: (1) expanding markets and commodification result in negative social impacts, (2) these impacts trigger the rise of social movements demanding better outcomes, (3) and this results in more government protections that address the negative impacts of commodification. As explained by Brechin and Fenner (2017: 407, 409), this pattern can also go back the other direction when protections are relaxed, resulting in a back-and-forth, or what Polanyi called the "double movement":

> The double movement, imagined as a swinging pendulum, swings repeatedly from economic liberalism to market regulation. From the environmental perspective, one can see the first swing of double movement as the push towards deregulation that produces environment degradation. In the swing back, worried individuals and groups create social movements to curb the damage through interventions, such as regulation by government. In response to these interventions, the swings continue and there are further free market enhancements at the request of industry that are once again met by countermovements. ... The fight over climate change becomes the modern illustration of yet another continuing pendulum struggle concerning environmental protection and economic liberalism, as outlined by Polanyi.

This depiction of social change suggests that things often get worse before they get better: the pendulum must swing far to one side before it is corrected. This depiction also suggests a possibly never-ending cycle of double movements, yet Polanyi believed that this cycle would end with the rise of the post–World War II welfare state, when it seemed socially decided that economies must be subordinated to social protections. This prediction was not correct, as the rise of market fundamentalism in the neoliberal era eroded many social protections, restoring the pattern. This might suggest that we are currently poised for a rise in protective measures, yet if governments fail to respond to social movements, where does it leave us? As Brechin and Fenner (2017) point out, while useful in many ways, Polanyi's narrative leaves many unanswered questions about countermovements, such as how they specifically succeed.

Sociologist Erik Olin Wright (2010, 2019) also developed a theory of social transformation based on more recent historical trends. In *Envisioning Real Utopias* (2010), Wright explains how certain elements are key to social transformation. A key step is identifying and challenging the forces of social reproduction, or *anti-reflexivity forces* (McCright and Dunlap 2010), as well as the ideologies used to maintain power. Another component is politicizing contradictions and inherent issues with the current system. This could include the evidence environmental sociologists and others have marshaled illustrating how we likely cannot address our environmental crisis in a growing economy and the moral implications of the status quo. Wright (2010) also discusses the importance of unexpected events in changing the playing field and the realm of possibility. For example, the Covid-19 pandemic is already showing signs of shifting social and political expectations and norms in new ways. Finally, there must be purposeful transformational strategies at play, usually led by social movements demanding change. Again, the strategies and actions of social movements are key. Movements can "erode" the system through simultaneously weakening the existing social order and introducing alternatives. In addition, a moral framing of an issue can be critical for successfully pushing forward positive social change (Wright 2019).

For our purposes, we can apply these insights to considering social movements and changes to effectively and justly address our environmental crisis. It should be noted that research on the "environmental movement" has largely focused on the Global North and groups largely consisting of upper- or middle-class white participants. However, there are also different types of environmental groups in the Global South, organized by poor and working-class people and increasingly focusing on addressing cases of environmental injustice (Satheesh 2020). Environmentalism need not be a class-based concern, yet environmentalism among the poor in the Global South may take on new forms in the context of the challenges faced. Again, this book primarily focuses on the Global North, where the high levels of production and consumption in affluent nations continue to push us deeper into a global environmental crisis. That said, environmental justice movements across the globe are increasingly focused on the responsibility of wealthy nations to act boldly and quickly to mitigate climate change and also to ensure protection for those in the Global South who are most vulnerable and will be most gravely impacted by what the United Nations calls a "climate apartheid."

While the "climate movement" has been around for a while, it became more visible following the People's Climate March in 2014 and through the work of Bill McKibben and 350.org's divestment campaign (Schifeling and Hoffman 2017). We also saw the March for Science in 2017, which illustrated a significant shift in the participation of scientists in climate activism (MacKendrick 2017, Fisher 2018). In many ways the climate movement was ephemeral in terms of political action until 2018. In 2018 we can clearly identify a legitimate movement, especially due to the rise of three social movement organizations: The Sunrise Movement, Extinction Rebellion, and Fridays for Future. For the latter two groups, demands for addressing the biodiversity crisis are also combined with demands to address climate change. In many cases these organizations coordinate and support each other, which has resulted in unprecedented participation.

Some people use the term "climate justice movement" instead of climate movement. While the term is used in different ways, in the context of discussions about national climate policy it refers to a particular focus on race and equality, which has taken on a greater importance in the climate movement in recent years. While there was more of an ecological modernization focus in the past (Caniglia et al. 2015), in 2020 for many organizations the focus and framing of climate proposals is on justice, protection, and equality through structural change. For example, many proposals for a Green New Deal in the US focus specifically on front-line communities and racial justice, as well as the redistribution of wealth, job guarantees, and universal health care. Justice remains a central focus of the US-based Sunrise Movement. While issues of justice and race once existed on the fringe of the climate movement, for many environmental groups and activists they have taken on a central role, especially after the Black Lives Matter protests in the spring and summer of 2020. Many environmental leaders in 2020 agree that any climate policy must take race, justice, and economic inequality into account.

Public Sociology: Pushing Forward a Climate Justice Agenda

If you are a news or podcast junkie, you may have noticed that Robert Bullard continues to be a leading voice that reporters and policymakers turn to in order to better understand environmental and climate justice. Bullard's list of media interviews is extensive and impressive (see https://drrobertbullard.com/news/), with recent interviews in top news sources focusing on the intersection of race, climate, and the Covid-19 pandemic. He continues to highlight how minority communities, who have already faced higher exposure to pollutants and are therefore more vulnerable, now face more climate impacts and higher fatalities from Covid-19. He explained in one interview that "COVID-19 is like a heat-seeking missile that is targeting the most vulnerable populations, and the bull's-eye is actually the environmental justice communities, the communities that are the poorest, that are the most polluted, that are the sickest when it comes to comorbidity" (Wilson et al. 2020).

Specific to climate policy, Bullard stated, "Planning has to be sensitive to the fact that communities and nations have different levels of wealth, health, and education. The goal for planning should be to build community resilience and provide an opportunity for people to bounce back both before and after a catastrophic event. ... Policy and plans should begin by understanding why people become vulnerable" (Bullard et al. 2016). Bullard remains a vocal advocate for front-line communities who face the greatest impacts from climate events, like Hurricane Katrina (Bullard 2018). He has also been working with climate movement organizations to inform a just plan for a Green New Deal. Those at the forefront of designing a Green New Deal have been consulting with Bullard to incorporate his experience and ensure that justice is a central component of any climate policy. Bullard argues that a just Green New Deal must not only protect front-line communities but that the most vulnerable citizens must have a seat at the table and be participants in the creation of a just climate response.

As the climate movement evolves, decisions within the movement as well as external factors will determine its success. What constitutes success? Within the movement, notions of success range between finally moving the dial on climate (doing something) to implementing technological and market-based reforms, to implementing a transformational climate program involving structural changes. While movements have less control over external factors, such as political openings and barriers, other conditions can be purposefully pursued, such as through Wright's (2010, 2019) "transformation strategies." In terms of decisions that are within the control of climate movement organizations, research suggests that the climate movement is more likely to be successful if it is nonviolent, sustained over time, focused on a moral framing of the issue, and demanding structural changes (Chenoweth and Stephan 2011, McAdam 2017). While we cannot predict their success, Extinction Rebellion, the Sunrise Movement, and Fridays for Future all continue to demand that governments take bold action to address our environmental crisis, and there are no signs of these groups giving up any time soon. We will briefly examine these efforts and the growing momentum of the climate movement.

Growing Momentum for Change

John Bellamy Foster has long argued that nothing short of an ecological revolution will be able to address the climate crisis and that such a revolution is highly unlikely. Yet in 2019 Foster states that we are seeing what "appears to be the beginnings of an ecological revolution, a new historical moment unlike any humanity has experienced" (Foster 2019). While he explains that the climate movement is up against powerful forces, he argues that the movement is now "on fire" in ways it has never been before. This is largely due to the rise of Extinction Rebellion, the Sunrise Movement, and Fridays for Future. As a timely example of social movement analysis, we will take a closer look at these efforts.

Following the release of the IPCC's 2018 special report, stating the critical importance of keeping average global temperature increases below 1.5 °C, the climate activist group Extinction Rebellion initiated a wave of protests and acts of civil disobedience in the UK that have been sustained over time and have spread internationally. The group claims that because governments have failed to take meaningful action on climate and biodiversity loss, people should rebel until governments respond. Extinction Rebellion has three demands: that governments (1) tell the truth about the climate and biodiversity crises, (2) enact legally binding policies to reduce carbon emissions to net zero by 2025 (while reducing total global resource use), and (3) create a democratic citizens' assembly to direct a wartime-level effort to address these crises. Extinction Rebellion UK's strategy involves civil disobedience and disrupting business-as-usual through occupying major sites in London for up to two weeks. In November 2018, over 6,000 activists shut down five major bridges in London and in April 2019 activists occupied five major London sites, turning them into camps with a carnival atmosphere, which resulted in over 1,100 arrests. In October 2019 they again shut down major sites around London, resulting in about 1,800 arrests. They plan to keep organizing rebellions and other interferences until their three demands are met. Dylan Bugden (2020) found that the civil disobedience actions of Extinction Rebellion have been highly influential in increasing public support for climate action.

In the US, the youth-led Sunrise Movement has been pressuring members of Congress to support the Green New Deal (GND) resolution, calling for net-zero emissions by 2050. Championed by progressive congresswoman Alexandria Ocasio-Cortez, the GND not only proposes extensive mitigation strategies but also targets inequality, racial injustice, and class exploitation. It has been called a product of social-democratic populism, targeting market fundamentalism and bringing forward a sweeping set of changes to transition to a new twenty-first century economy. The Sunrise Movement focuses on strategies to make the GND a political reality. Activists with Sunrise have been arrested outside of congressional offices and have launched a nationwide GND tour. Their efforts have not only raised public awareness but also made climate change a central issue for the 2020 elections. As a result of the Sunrise Movement's efforts, some version of a GND was supported by all of the leading 2020 Democratic presidential candidates and these candidates participated in a seven-hour CNN town hall devoted to discussing the climate crisis. An increasing number of progressive political challengers have emerged to run against Democrats who fail to support a GND.

The youth movement Fridays for Future carried out school strikes for climate action throughout late 2018; these increased in size and scale in 2019. The movement initiated with a single 15-year-old, Greta Thunberg, in Sweden and has expanded into global participation. The movement calls for youth school strikes on Fridays until governments meet the terms of the Paris Agreement. A letter from youth leaders states: "We finally need to treat the climate crisis as a crisis.

It is the biggest threat in human history and we will not accept the world's decision-makers' inaction that threatens our entire civilization." Their efforts resulted in the largest global strikes ever and the largest climate mobilizations to date. There were an estimated 1.6 million youth striking on March 15, 2019. In 2019 Fridays for Future asked adults to join them for the September 20 and 27 strikes. Extinction Rebellion and the Sunrise Movement also worked to organize strikes, along with other organizations such as 350.org, and the joint effort resulted in 6.5 to 7.5 million participants in more than 150 different countries. The young Fridays for Future student strikers are drawing attention to the failure of governments to protect their generation, and are exposing the intergenerational injustice of inaction. Their messages are transforming the framing of climate change from a political issue to a moral issue. They claim their future is being stolen because of greed and economic growth. At the September 23, 2019, United Nations Climate Change Summit, Greta Thunberg called for justice, stating, "We will not let them get away with this. The world is waking up and change is coming."

The aims and strategies of these three groups differ, yet they are largely synergistic. While Fridays for Future aims to pressure governments to act, to "unite behind the science," and to do what scientists say is necessary to stay below a 1.5°C global temperature increase, the Sunrise Movement has a more specific vision about how this should be done, as outlined in the GND resolution. The strategy of Sunrise is specifically to work within current US electoral politics. They believe the federal government is the only actor that can adopt the large-scale changes necessary, and the fastest way to take over government is through elections in existing political parties. Through focusing on Democratic primaries, voter registration, and GND town halls, Sunrise is attempting to bring the GND into the mainstream and create the political will to make it a reality. Sunrise activists continue to target members of the Democratic Party, asking them to support the GND and to not accept donations from fossil fuel interests.

Extinction Rebellion differs in terms of both goals and strategies. While Sunrise is working within the political system to bring forward climate change policies, Extinction Rebellion has strategically decided to attempt to be "beyond politics" and to avoid being associated with any political party in order to attract widespread and diverse participation. Co-founder Roger Hallam argues that climate change is about survival and is therefore a universal issue that farmers, businessmen, grandparents, and everyone should get involved in. Extinction Rebellion also claims that the political system is broken and cannot function properly to bring about the changes necessary. Instead, they call for a citizens' assembly of randomly selected citizens to hear expert testimonies and collectively decide on the best course of action. To get the attention and leverage needed to force the government to meet their demands, Extinction Rebellion UK focuses on disruption targeting government and finance in London. Through nonviolent acts of civil disobedience, shutting down transportation, and massive arrests, they aim to make the government cave to their demands.

As Extinction Rebellion, the Sunrise Movement, and Fridays for Future gained momentum, political analysts and journalists described their actions as historic, game-changing, and a turning point. Some of their work was brought to a sudden halt upon the arrival of the global Covid-19 pandemic, but each group found ways to keep active and they all continue to make plans for the future. Already it is clear that the efforts of the climate movement have increased awareness internationally, as seen through many public opinion polls in 2019 and 2020 showing that the majority of US and UK citizens, among others, support immediate climate action. In addition, in the US, Democratic political candidates are now being held to a higher standard and evaluated specifically on their climate plans and their support for a GND. There is no doubt these organizations have had an impact, yet it will take more pressure and increasing participation from citizens globally to push forward the structural changes necessary.

One sign of ripening conditions for social change is the shift in how the climate crisis is being framed, as it is more widely discussed as a moral issue. Fridays for Future and the participation of millions of children in school strikes has already had significant impacts on how the public views climate change. Greta Thunberg has been cited as having prophetic "moral clarity" that has reshaped the climate debate. Drawing increasing attention to this injustice, youth have also initiated lawsuits suing governments for robbing them of their future. In the US, the lawsuit *Juliana v. US* brought to attention the question of a constitutional right to a life free of climate change impacts. An international group of youth have also formally filed a human rights complaint with the United Nations, stating that under the UN Convention of The Rights of the Child, world leaders must protect all children from the catastrophic impacts of climate change. Youth activists are reframing climate change as an issue of generational injustice and fighting for their right to a livable future. As they demand that world leaders protect their future and "put people before profits," they continue to draw attention to the immorality of continuing with business as usual. This could be significant. Wright (2010, 2019) argues that most people are motivated by moral concerns rather than class or economic concerns. A shift toward a moral framing focused on intergenerational impacts could make the climate crisis be widely seen as a universal justice issue that is immoral to ignore.

Despite this momentum, there are clear challenges to success. This includes the rise of leaders in multiple countries who are opposed to climate action and continue to dismiss, ignore, and worsen climate impacts. Restoration of democracy and new political leaders willing to prioritize social and ecological well-being are key, but these are only some of the challenges the climate movement faces. As discussed previously, anti-reflexivity forces (McCright and Dunlap 2010) continue to oppose climate action, and fossil fuel, transportation, and other industrial sectors continue to put excessive funds into blocking even modest climate policies. In addition, Brulle and Norgaard (2019) explain how the idea of climate change results in "cultural trauma" that makes people not want to think about it and contributes to inaction. Thus, despite ample information, these emotional responses hinder action. Another contributor to inaction is a belief that we are doomed and it is already too late.

It will be critical that the climate movement counters "climate defeatism," or the acceptance of defeat and surrender of the climate struggle, as well as "climate fatalism," or the idea that there is only one possible climate future that we are powerless to influence. The power of the fossil fuel industry, lingering neoliberal ideology, and the realities of a captive political system continue to represent significant roadblocks to change. As a result of the daunting nature of these roadblocks, many people understandably have pessimistic, defeatist, and fatalistic views about addressing the climate crisis. However, in *Envisioning Real Utopias* (2010) Erik Olin Wright clearly explains the dangers of fatalism and cynicism. Wright warns that "fatalism poses a serious problem for people committed to challenging the injustices and harms of the existing social world, since fatalism and cynicism about the prospects for emancipatory change reduce the prospects for such change."

While it is too late to stop the climate impacts we are already experiencing and will experience in the near future, drastically reducing emissions now will reduce the likelihood of worst-case scenarios in the future. As explained by journalist David Wallace-Wells (2019):

> It is not a matter of "yes" or "no," ... Instead, it is a problem that gets worse over time the longer we produce greenhouse gas, and can be made better if we choose to stop. Which means that no matter how hot it gets, no matter how fully climate change transforms the planet and the way we live on it, it will always be the case that the next decade could contain more warming, and more suffering, or less warming and less suffering. Just how much is up to us, and always will be.

Some climate scientists have publicly argued that climate defeatism has become more dangerous than climate denial. Climate denial campaigns prevented early acceptance of and action on climate change. Climate defeatism has been called a new breed of climate denialism or "de-nihilism"— suggesting that action and even existence is meaningless and futile. However, propagating fatalist and defeatist views may also represent a strategy to impede climate policy and system change. It could be used as an excuse to focus solely on adaptation, as well as allowing the fossil fuel industry to further extract fossil fuel reserves and continue to reap vast profits. While the challenges for implementing effective climate policies are real and indeed daunting, climate defeatism and fatalism impede action and therefore only help to ensure the status quo.

While we cannot predict the future, there continues to be momentum to address escalating existential threats. While the Covid-19 pandemic may have temporarily derailed some efforts or distracted people from environmental concerns, there are efforts under way to attempt to combine pandemic relief with addressing the climate crisis. Already in some places such as Germany, "green" stimulus plans have been proposed to achieve multiple goals simultaneously. What Covid-19 is also illustrating is how continuing to prioritize economic growth before well-being results in more loss and suffering. For example, if governments in the US had prioritized well-being early in the pandemic, fatalities would have been much lower. State governments moved forward with reopening businesses, despite public opinion polls showing that the majority of Americans would have chosen to prioritize health (and lockdown) over the economy (*Newsweek* 2020). Similarly, the majority of Americans would prioritize addressing environmental issues over economic growth (Gallup Poll 2019). While these are clear indicators of ripening conditions for social change, the challenges ahead remain significant.

These circumstances suggest that there is much work to be done. As some environmental leaders have made clear, their goals must be long-term and they must have the endurance to keep working. Even a legal victory can be quickly overturned. If an issue is resolved in one place, it may emerge in another. In other words, it is important to accept that the fight will never truly end. There will always be ways to better protect and support social and ecological well-being. There will always be work to be done. This long-term outlook and acceptance of the need for endurance is also important for environmental sociologists. Even when we may feel defeated by specific outcomes, there is more work to be done. Thus, perseverance is critical.

Moving Forward in Environmental Sociology

Given the seriousness of the crisis we face, environmental sociology has never mattered more. As illustrated throughout this book, environmental sociologists continue to do research that is highly relevant to society. This includes work not only to push forward effective solutions to address existential threats, but also to identify and address environmental racism, injustice, toxic exposures, and other forms of systemic environmental harm. Despite the pressing nature of the global challenges we face, it is critical that our work continues to include all environmental issues. Regional issues will also increasingly be impacted and exacerbated by global warming and biodiversity loss and more work will be needed to understand these relationships and how to minimize all environmental impacts moving forward. Public sociology will only become more important as these impacts and their complexities unfold.

As demonstrated throughout this book, in many cases, research in environmental sociology is an example of public sociology. This trend will need to increase in the near future as our challenges intensify. Why should we do public sociology? In *Sociological Forum*, Andrew Jorgenson (2018: 1087) describes three reasons he participates in public sociology:

> First, I'm worried about the future of the planet and all of its human and nonhuman habitants, and since graduate school I've taken a problems-oriented approach in most of my research, scholarship, and teaching. Second, there is too much emphasis in policy and media venues on technological, behavioral, and market-based solutions to our global sustainability challenges, especially climate change, while downplaying the ways in which structural inequalities and power dynamics from the local to the global contribute to anthropogenic climate change and other environmental problems. Third, I've been encouraged to participate in these sorts of activities, and I've received very helpful guidance from friends and colleagues.

These reasons are enlightening and likely motivate many other scholars as well. Many of us are deeply concerned about the future of the planet. Also, as illustrated in this book, the current focus on "technological, behavioral, and market-based solutions" as the best solution pathways is not well supported by empirical evidence, is risky, and raises serious moral concerns. Using data to evaluate the viability of different solution pathways has been a critically important contribution from environmental sociologists. Public sociology is hard work and takes more time, yet it is rewarding and creates a community of scholar-activists and scholar-policymakers who can help steer a course toward positive change. In the coming years there will be many opportunities for socially relevant and socially necessary environmental research.

As environmental and social crises continue to unfold, and actions to address them, for the time being, remain insufficient, there are important emerging topical areas for environmental sociologists to examine. We will look at four in particular here, yet there are many more. First, as we go deeper into crisis we will experience not only physical impacts and losses but also emotional ones, and we need to further understand these emotional responses and how they encourage or constrain concern and activism. Second, there is an ongoing power struggle between those who support structural change and those who remain faithful to ideas of technological fixes, minor reforms, and market-based solutions. This struggle is not only important to study but we also need to identify and pull critical levers to open up pathways for positive change. Third, as environmental changes inevitably unfold we need to identify how best to adapt and be resilient. Communities and environmental groups are already working on ways to increase resilience and understanding how we can best support and protect communities is critical. Finally, a continued focus on justice will be necessary moving forward. As climate change and other impacts worsen, finding ways to protect the most vulnerable is essential.

Loss is always inevitable, yet many people are already bracing for the increasing losses we will experience due to global warming and biodiversity loss – our two escalating existential threats. In "The Sociology of Climate Change as a Sociology of Loss," Rebecca Elliott (2018: 328) clearly describes the role of loss materially, politically, and emotionally and makes a compelling case for future research to better understand "what climate change looks like when it hits the ground." Norgaard and Reed (2017) also illustrate some of the emotional impacts of environmental change in a North American indigenous community, revealing feelings of shame, anger, grief, and hopelessness. More of this work is critical moving forward. We need to understand not only physical impacts, but the emotions involved in being human in this time of loss. Elliott (2018: 329) explains that a focus on loss need not be pessimistic, as it is something that makes us fundamentally similar and can bring us closer together: "The shared experience of loss is something that emphatically connects humans—we often respond with sensitivity and generosity to the losses of others." Examples of assistance, support, and connection can be identified, examined, and encouraged. As more loss inevitably unfolds in the years to come, environmental sociologists can contribute to understanding how it reshapes society.

More work is also needed to understand how people emotionally respond to threats, and how these responses may impede support for change. There has been an increase not only in "climate grief" but also "climate anxiety"—or choosing avoidance and ignorance to protect oneself. There are an increasing number of self-help books to support those confronting and processing the emotions related to our existential precarity. Most argue that rather than falling into despair and inaction there is a moral imperative to face reality and fight to minimize the negative impacts to humans and other species. Norgaard (2011) and Brulle and Norgaard (2019) reveal how emotions play a key role in how people process and respond to the threat of climate change. As the climate movement and climate politics are increasingly reshaping the dominant frames and narratives, we must examine how these changes influence emotional responses, and specifically how people face the challenges of reality without falling into fatalistic forms of apathy and inaction. If we believe the only option is doom and gloom, it is very likely that is what we will get. We need to give more attention to alternative outcomes, as they are still possible and worth pursuing. Future work is necessary that illustrates possibilities and highlights alternative futures. This work is critically needed to spread ideas and visions of a very possible better future.

Second, as power struggles intensify we need to more deeply examine actors, strategies, tactics, and battlegrounds as solutions to our environmental crisis are increasingly debated. Will we go down the route of technological optimism and rely on solar geoengineering to "fix" climate change and on science to recreate the ecosystem services we now rely upon? As illustrated in this book, there are risks to such approaches, with vast moral implications. Another option, which is harder for most people to imagine, is the path of structural transformation to a more just, equitable, and sustainable social order. As we saw in the last chapter, there are viable strategies that can be pushed forward in synergistic ways to foster positive social change. Yet, "anti-reflexivity forces" (McCright and Dunlap 2010) remain powerful despite the scientific evidence and public opinion polls indicating the necessity of and support for bold action. Those in power attempt to maintain this power. These power dynamics must shift in order to preserve and protect life as we know it. This realization is growing among environmental activists, yet it needs to spread among the general public more broadly. More research is needed to understand the role of ideology in maintaining the status quo—and, more important, how we can counter the ideologies that stand in the way of efforts to address our environmental crisis effectively.

We know who the anti-reflexivity forces are, we know they have ample resources (e.g., Brulle 2018b), and we know they are actively working against structural changes that would negatively impact economic growth and wealth accumulation. We need to continue to expose these actors, their financial and political ties, and use this work to reduce corporate influence over our governments, strengthening our democracies. Already, exposing politicians for not representing their constituents has in some cases resulted in their failure to be re-elected. More research needs to study the dynamics of these power struggles and the role of media, money, ideology, and the suppression of voices and votes. As depicted by Antonio Gramsci (1971) long ago, we have opposing forces at play and strategic moves to gain dominance. The outcome of this struggle could not have more planetary importance. We need more research not only to document and better understand the complicated, multifaceted nature of these struggles but also to continue to expose who is acting and why, and to politicize what is at stake.

As of 2020, in addition to the environmental crisis, we also face multiple other intersecting social crises: a public health crisis (Covid-19), a racial justice crisis (the police killing of George Floyd and resulting protests), as well as economic inequality and a broken democracy. Research is needed to understand how these crises impact each other: for example, how climate, race, and health intersect, as well as which solution pathways might be able to address multiple crises at once. While these are indeed daunting crises, they reveal the need for structural changes and may together raise awareness enough to open up pathways for positive change. There are already formulated policy ideas aimed at addressing multiple social crises at once. Such opportunities and ideas need to be identified and politicized. In addition, environmental sociologists must continue to work with policymakers and organizations, designing pathways to create a more just and sustainable society.

Third, as Elliott (2018) indicates, more research is necessary to understand forms of connection, strength, and resilience moving forward. Even a future with the least possible impacts will require adaption, resilience, and supportive communities. Some activist groups have already created networks for support and building adaptive communities that strengthen their ability to face the challenges ahead. For example, one of Extinction Rebellion's foundational goals is to build a "regenerative culture." The group continues to plan acts of civil disobedience and to demand structural change, but they are simultaneously working to build a culture that increases their capacity to adapt to future climate impacts. Adaptation does not mean defeat, as their efforts to minimize warming through activism and civil disobedience continue. To fuel their ongoing work, Extinction Rebellion has support groups for activists to acknowledge and grieve the losses they are experiencing now and will likely experience in the future. They are also working to increase skills related to growing food and home provisioning as well as living with less and sharing more. These networks build resilience and also help to increase and sustain energy for ongoing efforts to demand change. As similar networks emerge and grow, environmental sociologists can examine these strategies for collective resistance and resilience and identify how people can come together and support each other in the face of hardship. Environmental sociologists must continue, and increase, efforts to expose and address environmental injustice, as those who are most vulnerable and least responsible continue to experience disproportionate impacts. This applies to local impacts as well as global patterns of disproportionate impacts. For example, African-American communities face a higher burden of harm from the intersection of risks due to pollution, climate, Covid-19, and systemic racism. These communities must be better protected and also given a leading role in designing better ways to ensure this protection. More work is needed to identify structural changes that can address multiple threats to vulnerable communities at once. We must seek solutions that are not only effective but just. Future work also needs to continue to identify barriers to addressing environmental justice and how to overcome these barriers. For example, Jill Harrison's (2015, 2017) research reveals some troubling issues with environmental justice work in organizations and government agencies, highlighting the need to unify definitions and strengthen approaches to environmental justice. At a global level, as climate impacts disproportionately affect the poor in the Global South, we must find ways to better protect at-risk populations. Global climate injustice will be difficult to address, but already work has revealed some of the drivers of unequal global exchange (Givens et al. 2019) as well as how injustices could be ameliorated by more equitable trade, debt forgiveness, and alternative pathways for "sustainable" development (Hickel 2017). Justice and equity at both the local and global scales must be given constant attention as we develop and implement solutions to address our environmental crisis.

Doing the Necessary Work

Those who decide to pursue a career in environmental sociology now do so at a critical time. Given the global and existential nature of the environmental crisis, we truly are in uncharted waters. While the existing theories, approaches, and debates in environmental sociology have evolved over time and made important contributions along the way, the questions that environmental sociologists examine have never mattered more. Identifying environmental impacts, the underlying drivers of these impacts, effective and just solutions, and pathways for social change have taken on unprecedented importance. This is why the work of environmental sociologists can be increasingly seen in journals such as *Nature Climate Change* and in *The New York Times* and *The Washington Post*. This level of public relevance and engagement has elevated environmental sociology to a very important area of study.

Environmental sociologists will continue to contribute empirical analyses and theoretical insights that help us to answer critical questions and support ongoing efforts to create a more just and sustainable world. There is much at stake, and there are significant moral implications associated with the paths we choose. Yet, no matter what unfolds in the near future, there is much work to be done. In doing this work, we must be honest about the realities, but not let the challenges ahead stop us from doing the necessary work.

Discussion Questions

1. Compare the different depictions of how social change occurs. What explanations do you find most compelling and why?
2. What would climate justice at a local and global scale look like?
3. Do you think we are witnessing the start of an "ecological revolution"? Why or why not?
4. What is "climate defeatism" and why is it important to address?
5. What do you think are the most inspiring examples of public sociology? Why?

Suggested Reading

Beck, U. (2016). *The metamorphosis of the world: How climate change is transforming our concept of the world.* Cambridge: Polity.

Brechin, S. R., & W. H. Fenner IV. (2017). Karl Polanyi's environmental sociology: a primer. *Environmental Sociology* 3(4): 404–413.

Brulle, R. J., & K. M. Norgaard. (2019). Avoiding cultural trauma: Climate change and social inertia. *Environmental Politics* 28(5): 886–908.

Caniglia, B. S., R. J. Brulle, & A. Szasz. (2015). Civil society, social movements, and climate change. *Climate Change and Society: Sociological Perspectives* 1: 235–268.

Elliott, R. (2018). The sociology of climate change as a sociology of loss. *European Journal of Sociology* 59(3): 301–337.

Foster, J. B. (2019). On fire this time. *Monthly Review* 71(6): 1–17.

Harrison, J. (2020). Environmental social movements. In *Twenty Lessons in Environmental Sociology*. Edited by K. A. Gould & T. L. Lewis. New York: Oxford University Press.

Lewis, T. (2020). Environmental movements in the Global South. In *Twenty Lessons in Environmental Sociology*. Edited by K. A. Gould & T. L. Lewis. New York: Oxford University Press.

Pellow, D. (2020). Politics by other greens: The importance of transnational environmental justice movement networks. In *Environmental Sociology: From Analysis to Action*. Edited by L. King and D. M. Auriffeille. Lanham, MD: Rowman & Littlefield.

Stuart, D., R. Gunderson, & B. Petersen. (2020). The climate crisis as a catalyst for emancipatory transformation: An examination of the possible. *International Sociology* 35(4): 433–456.

Wright, E. O. (2010). *Envisioning Real Utopias* (Vol. 98). London: Verso. Chapters 8–11.

References Cited

Alfredsson, E. C. (2004). "Green" consumption—no solution for climate change. *Energy* 29(4): 513–524.

Allen, S., T. Dietz, & A. M. McCright. (2015). Measuring household energy efficiency behaviors with attention to behavioral plasticity in the United States. *Energy Research & Social Science* 10: 133–140.

Allen, J. S., S. B. Longo, & T. E. Shriver. (2018). Politics, the state, and sea level rise: the treadmill of production and structural selectivity in North Carolina's coastal resource commission. *The Sociological Quarterly* 59(2): 320–337.

Baer, H. (2019). Toward democratic eco-socialism as the next world system. The Next System Project.

Beck, U. (1992). *Risk Society: Towards a New Modernity*. London: Sage.

Beck, U. (1996). Risk society and the provident state. In S. Lash, B. Szerszynski, & B. Wynne (Eds.), *Risk, Environment, & Modernity: Toward a New Ecology*. Thousand Oaks, CA: Sage.

Beck, U., W. Bonss, & C. Lau. (2003). The theory of reflexive modernization: Problematic, hypotheses and research programme. *Theory, Culture & Society* 20(2): 1–33.

Besek, J. F., & J. A. McGee. (2014). Introducing the ecological explosion: A cross-national analysis of invasive species and economic development. *International Journal of Sociology* 44(1): 75–93.

Besek, J. F., & R. York, R. (2019). Toward a sociology of biodiversity loss. *Social Currents* 6(3): 239–254.

Bolin, J. L., & L. C. Hamilton. (2018). The news you choose: News media preferences amplify views on climate change. *Environmental Politics* 27(3): 455–476.

Boström, M. (2020). The social life of mass and excess consumption. *Environmental Sociology* 6(3): 268–278.

Boström, M., R. Lidskog, & Y. Uggla. (2017). A reflexive look at reflexivity in environmental sociology. *Environmental Sociology* 3(1): 6–16.

Boström, M., & M. Klintman. (2019). Can we rely on "climate-friendly" consumption? *Journal of Consumer Culture* 19(3): 359–378.

Bourdieu, P. (1977). *Outline of a Theory of Practice.* Cambridge: Cambridge University Press.

Brechin, S. R., & W. H. Fenner, IV. (2017). Karl Polanyi's environmental sociology: A primer. *Environmental Sociology* 3(4): 404–413.

Brown, P. (2007). *Toxic Exposures: Contested Illnesses and the Environmental Health Movement.* New York: Columbia University Press.

Brulle, R. J. (2000). *Agency, Democracy, and Nature: The US Environmental Movement from a Critical Theory Perspective.* Cambridge, MA: MIT Press.

Brulle, R. J. (2014). Institutionalizing delay: foundation funding and the creation of US climate change counter-movement organizations. *Climatic Change* 122(4): 681–694.

Brulle, R. J. (2018a). Critical reflections on the march for science. *Sociological Forum* 33(1): 255–258.

Brulle, R. J. (2018b). The climate lobby: A sectoral analysis of lobbying spending on climate change in the USA, 2000 to 2016. *Climatic change* 149(3–4): 289–303.

Brulle, R. J., & J. T. Roberts. (2017). Climate misinformation campaigns and public sociology. *Contexts* 16(1): 78–79.

Brulle, R. J., & K. M. Norgaard. (2019). Avoiding cultural trauma: Climate change and social inertia. *Environmental Politics* 28(5): 886–908.

Bugden, D. (2020). Does climate protest work? Partisanship, protest, and sentiment pools. *Socius* 6.

Bullard, R. D. (Ed.). (1993). *Confronting Environmental Racism: Voices from the Grassroots.* Boston, MA: South End Press.

Bullard, R. D. (2008). *Dumping in Dixie: Race, Class, and Environmental Quality.* Boulder, CO: Avalon Publishing (Westview Press).

Bullard, R. D. (2018). The overlooked significance of place in law and policy: Lessons from Hurricane Katrina. In *Race, Place, and Environmental Justice After Hurricane Katrina* (pp. 71–84). London: Routledge.

Bullard, R. D. & G. S. Johnson. (2000). Environmentalism and public policy: Environmental justice: Grassroots activism and its impact on public policy decision making. *Journal of Social Issues* 56(3): 555–578.

Bullard, R. D., Gardezi, M., Chennault, C., & Dankbar, H. (2016). Climate Change and Environmental Justice: A Conversation with Dr. Robert Bullard. *Journal of Critical Thought and Praxis* 5(2).

Bulman, M. (2018). German workers win right to 28-hour week following industrial action. *Independent*. February 11, 2018. https://www.independent.co.uk/news/world/europe/german-workers-right-28hour-week-trade-union-industrial-action-ig-metall-a8205751.html

Burke, P. J., M. Shahiduzzaman, & D. I. Stern. (2015). Carbon dioxide emissions in the short run: the rate and sources of economic growth matter. *Global Environmental Change–Human and Policy Dimensions* 33: 109–121.

Burawoy, M. (2015). Facing an unequal world. *Current Sociology* 63(1): 5–34.

Buttel, F. H. (2000). Classical theory and contemporary environmental sociology. In *Environment and Global Modernity*. Edited by Gert Spaargaren, Arthur P. J. Mol, & Frederick H. Buttel (pp. 17–39). London: Sage.

Byskov, M. (2019). Climate change: Focusing on how individuals can help is very convenient for corporations. *The Conversation*. https://theconversation.com/climate-change-focusing-on-how-individuals-can-help-is-very-convenient-for-corporations-108546

Caniglia, B. S., R. J. Brulle, & A. Szasz. (2015). Civil society, social movements, and climate change. *Climate Change and Society: Sociological Perspectives* 1: 235–268.

Carfagna, L. B., E. A. Dubois, & C. Fitzmaurice. (2014). An emerging eco-habitus: The reconfiguration of high cultural capital practices among ethical consumers. *Journal of Consumer Culture* 14(2): 158–178.

Carmichael, J. T., & R. J. Brulle. (2017). Elite cues, media coverage, and public concern: an integrated path analysis of public opinion on climate change, 2001–2013. *Environmental Politics* 26(2): 232–252.

Carolan, M. S. (2005). Society, biology, and ecology: Bringing nature back into sociology's disciplinary narrative through critical realism. *Organization & Environment* 18(4): 393–421.

Catton, W. R., & R. Dunlap. (1978a). Environmental sociology–A new paradigm. *American Sociologist* 13: 41–49.

Catton, W. R., & R. Dunlap. (1978b). Paradigms, theories, and primacy of HEP-NEP distinction. *American Sociologist* 13: 256–259.

Catton, W. R., & R. Dunlap. (1980). A new ecological paradigm for post-exuberant sociology. *American Behavioral Scientist* 24: 15–47.

CBS News. (2019). Most Americans say climate change should be addressed now — CBS News poll. https://www.cbsnews.com/news/cbs-news-poll-most-americans-say-climate-change-should-be-addressed-now-2019-09-15/

Ceballos, G., P. R. Ehrlich, A. D. Barnosky, A. García, R. M. Pringle, & T. M. Palmer. (2015). Accelerated modern human-induced species losses: Entering the sixth mass extinction. *Science Advances* 1(5): 1400253.

Center for Behavior and the Environment. (2018). Climate Change Needs Behavior Change. https://www.rare.org/wp-content/uploads/2019/02/2018-CCNBC-Report.pdf

Center for Sustainable Systems, University of Michigan. (2019). Carbon Footprint Factsheet. Pub. No. CSS09-05.

Chenoweth, E., & M. J. Stephan. (2011). *Why civil resistance works: The strategic logic of nonviolent conflict*. New York: Columbia University Press.

Circle Economy. (2020). https://www.circularity-gap.world/2020

Clark, B. (2002). The indigenous environmental movement in the United States: Transcending borders in struggles against mining, manufacturing, and the capitalist state. *Organization & Environment* 15(4): 410–442.

Clark, B., & J. B. Foster. (2001). William Stanley Jevons and the Coal Question: an introduction to Jevons's "Of the Economy of Fuel". *Organization & Environment* 14(1): 93–98.

Clark, B., & R. York. (2005). Carbon metabolism: Global capitalism, climate change, and the biospheric rift. *Theory and Society* 34(4): 391–428.

Clark, B., A. K. Jorgenson, & J. Kentor. (2010). Militarization and energy consumption: A test of treadmill of destruction theory in comparative perspective. *International Journal of Sociology* 40(2): 23–43.

Clark, B., & A. K. Jorgenson. (2012). The treadmill of destruction and the environmental impacts of militaries. *Sociology Compass* 6(7): 557–569.

Clausen, R., & B. Clark. (2005). The metabolic rift and marine ecology: An analysis of the ocean crisis within capitalist production. *Organization & Environment* 18(4): 422–444.

Clement, M. T. (2011). The Jevons paradox and anthropogenic global warming: A panel analysis of state-level carbon emissions in the United States, 1963–1997. *Society & Natural Resources* 24(9): 951–961.

Collins, M., S. Pulver, D. Hill, & B. Manski. (2020). Characterizing disproportionality in facility-level toxic releases in US manufacturing, 1998–2012. *Environmental Research Letters* 15(6).

Collins, M. B., I. Munoz, & J. JaJa. (2016). Linking 'toxic outliers' to environmental justice communities. *Environmental Research Letters* 11(1): 015004.

Cordner, A. (2016). *Toxic Safety: Flame Retardants, Chemical Controversies, and Environmental Health*. New York: Columbia University Press.

Cordner, A., & P. Brown. (2015). A multisector alliance approach to environmental social movements: flame retardants and chemical reform in the United States. *Environmental Sociology* 1(1): 69–79.

Cordner, A., L. Richter, & P. Brown. (2019). Environmental chemicals and public sociology: Engaged scholarship on highly fluorinated compounds. *Environmental Sociology* 5(4): 339–351.

Czech, B., J. H. Mills Busa, & R. M. Brown. (2012). Effects of economic growth on biodiversity in the United States. *Natural Resources Forum* 36(3): 160–166.

Daly, H. (2013). A further critique of growth economics. *Ecological Economics* 88: 20–24.

Denny, R., & S. Marquart-Pyatt. (2019). Environmental sustainability in Africa: What drives the ecological footprint over time? *Sociology of Development* 4(1): 119–144.

Dickman, A., & G. Skinner. (2019). from Ipsos MORI. https://www.ipsos.com/ipsos-mori/en-uk/concern-about-climate-change-reaches-record-levels-half-now-very-concerned

Dietz, T. (2015). Altruism, self-interest, and energy consumption. *Proceedings of the National Academy of Sciences* 112(6): 1654–1655.

Dietz, T. (2017). Drivers of human stress on the environment in the twenty-first century. *Annual Review of Environment and Resources* 42: 189–213.

Dietz, T., & E. A. Rosa. (1994). Rethinking the environmental impacts of population, affluence and technology. *Human Ecology Review* 1(2), 277–300.

Dietz, T., & E. A. Rosa. (1997). Effects of population and affluence on CO_2 emissions. *Proceedings of the National Academy of Sciences* 94(1), 175–179.

Dietz, T., E. A. Rosa, & R. York. (2007). Driving the human ecological footprint. *Frontiers in Ecology and the Environment* 5(1), 13–18.

Dietz, T., G. T. Gardner, J. Gilligan, P. C. Stern, & M. P. Vandenbergh. (2009). Household actions can provide a behavioral wedge to rapidly reduce US carbon emissions. *Proceedings of the National Academy of Sciences* 106(44): 18452–18456.

Dietz, T., & C. T. Whitley. (2018). Environmentalism, norms, and identity. *Proceedings of the National Academy of Sciences* 115(49): 12334–12336.

Dietz, T., R. L. Shwom, & C. T. Whitley. (2020). Climate change and society. *Annual Review of Sociology* 46.

Dunlap, R. E., & W. R. Catton. (1979). Environmental sociology. *Annual Review of Sociology* 5: 243–273.

Dunlap, R. E., & W. R. Catton. (1983). What environmental sociologists have in common. *Sociological Inquiry* 53: 113–135.

Dunlap, R. E., & A. M. McCright. (2011). Organized climate change denial. *The Oxford Handbook of Climate Change and Society* 1: 144–160.

Dunlap, R. E., & A. M. McCright. (2015). Challenging climate change: The denial countermovement. In R. E. Dunlap & R. J. Brulle (eds.) *Climate Change and Society: Sociological Perspectives* (pp. 300–332). New York: Oxford University Press.

Easterlin, R. A., L. A. Mcvey, M. Switek, O. Sawangfa, & J. S. Zweig. (2010). The happiness-income paradox revisited. *Proceedings of the National Academy of Sciences of the United States of America* 107 (52): 22463–22468.

Economist Intelligence Unit. (2019). *Democracy index 2018: me too. Political participation, protest and democracy.* London: Economist Intelligence Unit. https://www.eiu.com/public/topical_report.aspx?campaignid=Democracy2018

Elliott, R. (2018). The sociology of climate change as a sociology of loss. *European Journal of Sociology/Archives Européennes de Sociologie* 59(3): 301–337.

Environmental Justice Foundation (2020). https://ejfoundation.org/

Environmental Protection Agency (2020). https://www.epa.gov/environmentaljustice

Fasenfest, D. (2019). A neoliberal response to an urban crisis: Emergency management in Flint, MI. *Critical Sociology* 45(1): 33–47.

Feng, K., S. J. Davis, L. Sun, & K. Hubacek. (2015). Drivers of the US CO_2 emissions 1997–2013. *Nature communications* 6: 7714.

Fisher, D. R. (2018). Scientists in the Resistance. *Sociological Forum* 33(1): 247–250.

Fisher, D. R., & A. K. Jorgenson. (2019). Ending the stalemate: Toward a theory of anthro-shift. *Sociological Theory* 37(4): 342–362.

Fiske, S., K. Hubacek, A. Jorgenson, J. Li, T. McGovern, T. Rick, J. Schor, W. Solecki, R. York, & A. Zycherman. (2018). Drivers and responses: Social science perspectives on climate change, part 2. Washington, DC: USGCRP Social Science Coordinating Committee.

Fitzgerald, J. B., A. K. Jorgenson, & B. Clark. (2015). Energy consumption and working hours: a longitudinal study of developed and developing nations, 1990–2008. *Environmental Sociology* 1(3): 213–223.

Fitzgerald, J. B., J. B. Schor, & A. K. Jorgenson. (2018). Working hours and carbon dioxide emissions in the United States, 2007–2013. *Social Forces* 96(4): 1851–1874.

Foster, J. B. (1999). Marx's theory of metabolic rift: Classical foundations for environmental sociology. *American Journal of Sociology* 105(2): 366–405.

Foster, J. B. (2013). Why ecological revolution. In King, L. and D. M. Auriffeille (Eds.) *Environmental sociology: From analysis to action* (pp. 35–48). London: Rowman and Littlefield.

Foster, J. B. (2019). On fire this time. *Monthly Review*. https://monthlyreview.org/2019/11/01/on-fire-this-time/

Foster, J. B., B. Clark, & R. York. (2011). *The Ecological Rift: Capitalism's War on the Earth*. New York: NYU Press.

Foster, J. B., & B. Clark. (2018). The robbery of nature. *Monthly Review* 70(3): 1–20.

Freudenburg, W. R. (2006). Environmental degradation, disproportion-ality, and the double diversion: Reaching out, reaching ahead, and reaching beyond. *Rural Sociology* 71(1): 3–32.

Freudenburg, W. R., S. Frickel, & R. Gramling. (1995). Beyond the nature/society divide: learning to think about a mountain. *Sociological Forum* 10 (3): 361–392.

Freudenburg, W. R., L. J. Wilson, & D. J. O'Leary. (1998). Forty years of spotted owls? A longitudinal analysis of logging industry job losses. *Sociological Perspectives* 41(1): 1–26.

Galbraith, K. (1958). *The Affluent Society*. Boston: Houghton Mifflin.

Galli Robertson, A. M., & M. B. Collins. (2019). Super emitters in the United States coal-fired electric utility industry: Comparing disproportionate emissions across facilities and parent companies. *Environmental Sociology* 5(1): 70–81.

Gallup Poll. (2019). https://news.gallup.com/poll/248243/preference-environment-economy-largest-2000.aspx

Ghosh, S. K., ed. (2020). *Circular Economy: Global Perspective*. Frankfurt: Springer Verlag.

Givens, J. E., B. Clark, & A. K. Jorgenson. (2016). Strengthening the ties between environmental sociology and sociology of development. *The Sociology of Development Handbook* (pp. 69–94). Berkeley, CA: University of California Press.

Givens, J. E., X. Huang, & A. K. Jorgenson. (2019). Ecologically unequal exchange: A theory of global environmental injustice. *Sociology Compass* 13(5): e12693.

Global Footprint Network. (2019). www.globalfootprintnetwork.org

Goldstein, B., D. Gounaridis, & J. P. Newell. (2020). The carbon footprint of household energy use in the United States. *Proceedings of the National Academy of Sciences* 117(32): 19122–19130.

Gorz, A. (1968). Reform and revolution. Socialist Register. https://socialistregister.com/index.php/srv/article/view/5272

Gotham, K. F. (2016). Coastal restoration as contested terrain: Climate change and the political economy of risk reduction in Louisiana. *Sociological Forum* 31: 787–806.

Gould, K. A. (2015). Slowing the nanotechnology treadmill: impact science versus production science for sustainable technological devel-opment. *Environmental Sociology* 1(3): 143–151.

Gould, K. A., D. N. Pellow, & A. Schnaiberg. (2004). Interrogating the treadmill of production: Everything you wanted to know about the treadmill but were afraid to ask. *Organization & Environment* 17(3): 296–316.

Gould, K. A., & T. L. Lewis. (2009). *Twenty Lessons in Environmental Sociology*. New York: Oxford University Press.

Gramsci, A. (1971). *The Prison Notebooks* (Volumes 1, 2 & 3). New York: Columbia University Press.

Green, A. & M. Scott Cato. (2018). Facts about our ecological crisis are incontrovertible: we must take action. *The Guardian.* October 26, 2018. https://www.theguardian.com/environment/2018/oct/26/facts-about-our-ecological-crisis-are-incontrovertible-we-must-take-action

Greenpeace. (2020). https://www.greenpeace.org/usa/issues/environmental-justice/

Griner, D. (2017). 18 Bullish Stats About the State of U.S. Advertising. *Adweek.* https://www.adweek.com/agencies/18-bullish-stats-about-the-state-of-u-s-advertising/

Grunwald, A. (2018). Diverging pathways to overcoming the environmental crisis: A critique of eco-modernism from a technology assessment perspective. *Journal of Cleaner Production* 197: 1854–1862.

Gunderson, R. (2014). Problems with the defetishization thesis: ethical consumerism, alternative food systems, and commodity fetishism. *Agriculture and Human Values* 31(1): 109–117.

Gunderson, R. (2015). Environmental sociology and the Frankfurt School 1: Reason and capital. *Environmental Sociology* 1(3): 224–235.

Gunderson, R. (2016). Environmental sociology and the Frankfurt School 2: Ideology, techno-science, reconciliation. *Environmental Sociology* 2(1): 64–76.

Gunderson, R. (2017). Ideology critique for the environmental social sciences: What reproduces the treadmill of production? *Nature and Culture* 12(3): 263–289.

Gunderson, R. (2019). Work time reduction and economic democracy as climate change mitigation strategies: Or why the climate needs a renewed labor movement. *Journal of Environmental Studies and Sciences* 9(1): 35–44.

Gunderson, R. (2020). Dialectics facing prehistoric catastrophe: Merely possible climate change solutions. *Critical Sociology* 46(4–5): 605–621.

Gunderson, R., D. Stuart, & B. Petersen. (2018). Ideological obstacles to effective climate policy: The greening of markets, technology, and growth. *Capital & Class* 42(1): 133–160.

Gunderson, R., D. Stuart, & B. Petersen. (2019). Materialized ideology and environmental problems: The cases of solar geoengineering and agricultural biotechnology. *European Journal of Social Theory* 13.

Hagmann, D., E. H. Ho, & G. Loewenstein. (2019). Nudging out support for a carbon tax. *Nature Climate Change* 9(6): 484–489.

Hall, C. A., J. G. Lambert, & S. B. Balogh. (2014). EROI of different fuels and the implications for society. *Energy Policy* 64: 141–152.

Hannigan, J. (2014). *Environmental Sociology.* London: Routledge.

Hardin, G. (1968). The tragedy of the commons. *Science* 162(3859): 1243–1248.

Harlan, S. L., D. N. Pellow, J. T. Roberts, S. E. Bell, W. G. Holt, & J. Nagel. (2015). Climate justice and inequality. *Climate Change and Society: Sociological Perspectives*: 127–163.

Harper, A. (2017). Germany's biggest union is fighting for a 28 hour working week – here's how the UK could follow suit. *The Independent*, October 12. https://www.independent.co.uk/voices/four-day-working-week-german-union-28-hours-uk-fight-for-the-same-a7996261.html.

Harrison, J. L. (2011). *Pesticide Drift and the Pursuit of Environmental Justice*. Cambridge, MA: MIT Press.

Harrison, J. L. (2014). Neoliberal environmental justice: Mainstream ideas of justice in political conflict over agricultural pesticides in the United States. *Environmental Politics* 23(4): 650–669. doi:10.1080/09644016.2013.877558.

Harrison, J. L. (2015). Coopted environmental justice? Activists' roles in shaping EJ policy implementation. *Environmental Sociology* 1(4): 241–255.

Harrison, J. L. (2016). Bureaucrats' tacit understandings and social movement policy implementation: Unpacking the deviation of agency environmental justice programs from EJ movement priorities. *Social Problems* 63(4): 534–553.

Harrison, J. L. (2017). "We do ecology, not sociology": Interactions among bureaucrats and the undermining of regulatory agencies' environmental justice efforts. *Environmental Sociology* 3(3): 197–212.

Harvey, C. (2016). This could be a completely different strategy for tackling the world's carbon emissions. July 7, 2016. *The Washington Post*. https://www.washingtonpost.com/news/energy-environment/wp/2016/07/07/this-could-be-a-completely-different-strategy-for-tackling-the-worlds-carbon-emissions/?noredirect=on

Harvey, F. (2020). Lockdown triggers dramatic fall in global carbon emissions. *The Guardian*, May 19, 2020. https://www.theguardian.com/environment/2020/may/19/lockdowns-trigger-dramatic-fall-global-carbon-emissions

Heron, K. (2020). ROAR Roundtable: COVID-19 and the Climate Crisis. https://www.resilience.org/stories/2020-06-25/roar-roundtable-covid-19-and-the-climate-crisis/

Hickel, J. (2017). *The Divide: A Brief Guide to Global Inequality and Its Solutions*. New York: Random House.

Hickel, J., & G. Kallis. (2019). Is green growth possible?. *New Political Economy* 25(4): 469–486.

Hill, T. D., & A. Jorgenson. (2018). Bring out your dead! A study of income inequality and life expectancy in the United States, 2000–2010. *Health & Place* 49: 1–6.

Houser, M., D. Stuart, & M. Carolan. (2017). Is seeing believing? Applying a realist framework to examine agriculture and climate change. *Environmental Sociology* 3(4): 321–336.

IPBES. (2019). Summary for policymakers of the global assessment report on biodiversity and ecosystem services of the Intergovernmental Science-Policy Platform on Biodiversity and Ecosystem Services. S. Díaz, et al. (eds.). IPBES secretariat, Bonn, Germany. 56.

IPCC Special Report 1.5: IPCC. (2018). Global warming of 1.5 degrees C. http://www.ipcc.ch/report/sr15/

Ipsen, A. (2016). Manufacturing a natural advantage: Capturing place-based technology rents in the genetically modified corn seed industry. *Environmental Sociology* 2(1): 41–52.

Ivanova, D., & R. Wood. (2020). The unequal distribution of household carbon footprints in Europe and its link to sustainability. *Global Sustainability* 3.

Jensen, D. (2009). Forget shorter showers. *Orion Magazine.* https://orionmagazine.org/article/forget-shorter-showers/

Jorgenson, A. K. (2003). Consumption and environmental degradation: A cross-national analysis of the ecological footprint. *Social Problems* 50(3): 374–394.

Jorgenson, A. K. (2016). The sociology of ecologically unequal exchange, foreign investment dependence and environmental load displacement: Summary of the literature and implications for sustainability. *Journal of Political Ecology* 32: 334–49.

Jorgenson, A. K. (2018). Broadening and deepening the presence of environmental sociology. *Sociological Forum* 33(4): 1086–1091.

Jorgenson, A. K., J. Rice, & J. Crowe. (2005). Unpacking the ecological footprint of nations. *International Journal of Comparative Sociology* 46(3): 241–260.

Jorgenson, A. K., & B. Clark. (2012). Are the economy and the environment decoupling? A comparative international study, 1960–2005. *American Journal of Sociology* 118(1): 1–44.

Jorgenson, A. K., & B. Clark. (2016). The temporal stability and developmental differences in the environmental impacts of militarism: the treadmill of destruction and consumption-based carbon emissions. *Sustainability Science* 11(3): 505–514.

Jorgenson, A., W. Longhofer, & D. Grant. (2016b). Disproportionality in power plants' carbon emissions: a cross-national study. *Scientific Reports* 6: 28661.

Jorgenson, A. K., J. B. Schor, K. Knight, & X. Huang. (2016a). Domestic inequality and carbon emissions in comparative perspective. *Sociological Forum* 31 (S1): 770–86.

Jorgenson, A., J. Schor, J., & X. Huang. (2017). Income inequality and carbon emissions in the United States: a state-level analysis, 1997–2012. *Ecological Economics* 134: 40–48.

Jorgenson, A. K., S. Fiske, K. Hubacek, J. Li, T. McGovern, T. Rick, ... & A. Zycherman. (2019). Social science perspectives on drivers of and responses to global climate change. *Wiley Interdisciplinary Reviews: Climate Change* 10(1): e554.

Kallis, G. (2018). *Degrowth*. Newcastle upon Tyne: Agenda Publishing.
Kallis, G. (2019). Capitalism, Socialism, Degrowth: A Rejoinder. *Capitalism Nature Socialism* 30(2): 267–273.
Kallman, M. E., & S. Frickel. (2019). Power to the people: industrial transition movements and energy populism. *Environmental Sociology* 5(3): 255–268.
Kaup, B. Z. (2015). Markets, nature, and society: embedding economic & environmental sociology. *Sociological Theory*: 33(3): 280–296.
Klein, N. (2015). *This Changes Everything: Capitalism vs. the Climate*. New York: Simon and Schuster.
Klinenberg, E., M. Araos, M., & L. Koslov. (2020). Sociology and the climate crisis. *Annual Review of Sociology* 46: 649–669.
Knight, K. W. (2016). Public awareness and perception of climate change: a quantitative cross-national study. *Environmental Sociology* 2(1): 101–113.
Knight, K., & J. Schor. (2014). Economic growth and climate change: A cross-national analysis of territorial and consumption-based CO_2 emissions in the OECD. *Sustainability* 6(6): 3722–3731.
Knight, K., E. Rosa, & J. Schor. (2013). Could working less reduce pressures on the environment? A cross-national panel analysis of OECD countries, 1970–2007. *Global Environmental Change* 23: 691–700.
Knight, K. W., J. B. Schor, & A. K. Jorgenson. (2017). Wealth inequality and carbon emissions in high-income countries. *Social Currents* 4(5): 403–412.
Krings, A., D. Kornberg, & E. Lane. (2019). Organizing under austerity: how residents' concerns became the Flint water crisis. *Critical Sociology* 45(4–5): 583–597.
Larrain, J. (1979). *The Concept of Ideology*. Athens: University of Georgia Press.
Lenton, T. M., J. Rockström, O. Gaffney, S. Rahmstorf, K. Richardson, W. Steffen, & H. J. Schellnhuber. (2019). Climate tipping points—too risky to bet against. *Nature* (575): 592–595.
Lewis, T. L. (2009). Environmental movements in the Global South. In Gould, K. A., & T. L. Lewis, *Twenty Lessons in Environmental Sociology*. New York: Oxford University Press.
Lidskog, R., & G. Sundqvist. (2018). Environmental expertise. In *Environment and Society* (pp. 167–186). London: Palgrave Macmillan.
Lockie, S. (2015). What is environmental sociology? *Environmental Sociology* 1(3): 139–142.
Lockie, S. (2018). Privilege and responsibility in environmental justice research. *Environmental Sociology*: 175–180.
Longo, S., & R. York. (2008). Agricultural exports and the environment: A cross-national study of fertilizer and pesticide consumption. *Rural Sociology* 73(1): 82–104.
Longo, S. B., & R. Clausen. (2011). The tragedy of the commodity:

The overexploitation of the Mediterranean bluefin tuna fishery. *Organization and Environment* 24(3): 312–328.

Longo, S. B., R. Clausen, & B. Clark. (2015). *The Tragedy of the Commodity: Oceans, Fisheries, and Aquaculture*. New Brunswick, NJ: Rutgers University Press.

Lorenzen, J. A. (2014). Green consumption and social change: debates over responsibility, private action, and access. *Sociology Compass* 8(8): 1063–1081.

Löwy, M. (2006). Why ecosocialism: For a red-green future. Great Transition Initiative. https://greattransition.org/publication/why-ecosocialism-red-green-future

Lowrey, A. (2019). The case against paper straws. *The Atlantic*: https://www.theatlantic.com/ideas/archive/2019/08/paper-straws-wont-stop-climate-change/596302/

MacKendrick, N. (2010). Media framing of body burdens: Precautionary consumption and the individualization of risk. *Sociological Inquiry* 80(1): 126–149.

MacKendrick, N. (2014). More work for mother: Chemical body burdens as a maternal responsibility. *Gender & Society* 28(5): 705–728.

MacKendrick, N. (2017). Out of the labs and into the streets: scientists get political. *Sociological Forum*, 32(4): 896–902.

MacKendrick, N. (2018). *Better Safe than Sorry: How Consumers Navigate Exposure to Everyday Toxics*. Berkeley: University of California Press.

MacKendrick, N., & L. M. Stevens. (2016). Taking back a little bit of control: Managing the contaminated body through consumption. *Sociological Forum* 31 (2): 310-329.

Malcom, J., M. W. Schwartz, M. Evansen, W. J. Ripple, S. Polask, L. R. Gerber … & J. R. Miller. (2019). Solve the biodiversity crisis with funding. *Science* 365(6459): 1256–1256.

Malin, S. A., & S. S. Ryder. (2018). Developing deeply intersectional environmental justice scholarship. *Environmental Sociology* 4(1): 1–7.

Marcuse, H. (1964). *One-dimensional man: The ideology of advanced industrial society*. Boston: Beacon.

Marcuse, H. (1967). The End of Utopia. Lecture. https://www.marxists.org/reference/archive/marcuse/works/1967/end-utopia.htm

Markle, G. (2019). Understanding pro-environmental behavior in the US: Insights from grid-group cultural theory and cognitive sociology. *Sustainability* 11(2): 532.

Marlon, J., P. Howe, M. Mildenberger, A. Leiserowitz, & X. Wang. (2020). Yale's website for climate opinion data. https://climatecommunication.yale.edu/visualizations-data/ycom-us/

Marquart-Pyatt, S. T., A. M. McCright, T. Dietz, & R. E. Dunlap. (2014). Politics eclipses climate extremes for climate change perceptions. *Global Environmental Change* 29: 246–257.

McAdam, D. (2017). Social movement theory and the prospects for climate change activism in the United States. *Annual Review of Political Science* 20: 189–208

McCormick, S., Brown, P., & Zavestoski, S. (2003). The personal is scientific, the scientific is political: the public paradigm of the environmental breast cancer movement. *Sociological Forum* 18(4): 545–576.

McCright, A. M., K. Dentzman, M. Charters, & T. Dietz. (2013). The influence of political ideology on trust in science. *Environmental Research Letters* 8(4): 044029.

McCright, A. M., & R. E. Dunlap. (2010). Anti-reflexivity. *Theory, Culture & Society* 27(2–3): 100–133.

McCright, A. M., & R. Dunlap. (2015). Challenging climate change: The denial countermovement. In R. E. Dunlap & R. J. Brulle (eds.) *Climate Change and Society: Sociological Perspectives.* New York: Oxford University Press.

McKinzie, A. E. (2019). You don't miss it 'til it's gone: Insecurity, place, and the social construction of the environment. *Environmental Sociology* 1–11.

Mohai, P. (2018). Environmental justice and the Flint water crisis. *Michigan Sociological Review* 32: 1–41.

Mohai, P., D. Pellow, & J. T. Roberts. (2009). Environmental justice. *Annual Review of Environment and Resources* 34: 405–430.

Mol, A. P. J., & G. Spaargaren. (2000). Ecological modernization theory in debate: A review. *Environmental Politics* 9: 17–49.

Mol, A. P., G. Spaargaren, & D. A. Sonnenfeld. (2013). Taking stock, moving forward. *Routledge International Handbook of Social and Environmental Change* 2.

Molotsky, I. (1988). Reagan Vetoes Bill Putting Limits On TV Programming for Children. *The New York Times.* November 7, 1988. https://www.nytimes.com/1988/11/07/us/reagan-vetoes-bill-putting-limits-on-tv-programming-for-children.html

Moran, D., R. Wood, E. Hertwich, K. Mattson, J. F. Rodriguez, K. Schanes, & J. Barrett. (2018). Quantifying the potential for consumer-oriented policy to reduce European and foreign carbon emissions. *Climate Policy*: 1–11.

Newsweek. (2020). https://www.newsweek.com/majority-americans-support-closing-down-economy-again-over-coronavirus-spike-poll-

Norgaard, K. M. (2011). *Living in Denial: Climate Change, Emotions, and Everyday Life.* Cambridge, MA: MIT Press.

Norgaard, K. M., & R. Reed, R. (2017). Emotional impacts of environmental decline: What can Native cosmologies teach sociology about emotions and environmental justice? *Theory and Society* 46(6): 463–495.

Norgaard, K. M., Reed, R., & Van Horn, C. (2011). Institutional Racism, Hunger and Nutritional Justice on the Klamath. In A. H. Alkon & J. Agyeman (eds.), *Cultivating Food Justice: Race, Class and Sustainability.* Cambridge, MA: MIT Press.

Norgaard, K. M. (2014). Karuk Traditional Ecological Knowledge and the Need for Knowledge Sovereignty. https://karuktribeclimate changeprojects.com/about/karuk-tek-knowledge-sovereignty/

Norgaard, K. M. (2016). Karuk Tribe Climate Vulnerability Assessment. https://karuktribeclimatechangeprojects.com/climate-vulnerabilty-assessment/

Norgaard, K. M. & W. Tripp. (2019). Karuk Climate Adaptation Plan. https://karuktribeclimatechangeprojects.com/climate-adaptation-plan/

Norgaard, K. M., Reed, R., & Bacon, J. M. (2017). How Environmental Decline Restructures Indigenous Gender Practices: What Happens to Karuk Masculinity When There Are No Fish? *Sociology of Race and Ethnicity* 4(1). https://doi.org/10.1177/2332649217706518.

O'Connor, J. (1988). Capitalism, nature, socialism a theoretical introduction. *Capitalism, Nature, Socialism* (1): 11–38.

Olofsson, A., Öhman, S. & Nygren, K.G. (2016). An intersectional risk approach for environmental sociology. *Environmental Sociology* 2(4): 346–354.

O'Neill, D. W. (2012). Measuring progress in the degrowth transition to a steady state economy. *Ecological Economics* 84: 221–231.

O'Neill, D. W., A. L. Fanning, W. F. Lamb, & J. K. Steinberger. (2018). A good life for all within planetary boundaries. *Nature Sustainability* 1(2).

Oswald, Y., A. Owen, & J. K. Steinberger. (2020). Large inequality in international and intranational energy footprints between income groups and across consumption categories. *Nature Energy* 5(3): 231–239.

Oxfam. 2015. Extreme Carbon Inequality. https://www-cdn.oxfam.org/s3fs-public/file_attachments/mb-extreme-carbon-inequality-021215-en.pdf

Parrique T., J. Barth, F. Briens, C. Kerschner, A. Kraus-Polk, A. Kuokkanen, & J. H. Spangenberg. (2019). Decoupling debunked: Evidence and arguments against green growth as a sole strategy for sustainability. European Environmental Bureau.

Park, L. S., & D. N. Pellow. (2011). *The Slums of Aspen: Immigrants vs. the Environment in America's Eden.* New York: New York University Press.

Pellow, D. N. (2002). *Garbage Wars: The Struggle for Environmental Justice in Chicago.* Cambridge, MA: MIT Press.

Pellow, D. N. (2005). Environmental racism: Inequality in a toxic world. In M. Romero & E. Margolis (Eds.) *The Blackwell Companion to Social Inequalities* (pp. 47–64). Malden, MA: Blackwell.

Pellow, D. N. (2007). *Resisting Global Toxics: Transnational Movements for Environmental Justice.* Cambridge, MA: MIT Press.

Pellow, D. N. (2011). Politics by other greens: The importance of transnational environmental justice movement networks. In J. Carmin

& J. Agyeman (Eds.) *Environmental Inequalities Beyond Borders: Local Perspectives on Global Injustices* (pp. 247–266). Cambridge, MA: The MIT Press.

Polanyi, K. 2001 (1944). *The Great Transformation: The Political and Economic Origins of Our Time*. Boston: Beacon Press.

Pullinger, M. (2014). Working time reduction policy in a sustainable economy: Criteria and options for its design. *Ecological Economics* 103: 11–19.

Ransan-Cooper, H. (2016). The role of human agency in environmental change and mobility: a case study of environmental migration in Southeast Philippines. *Environmental Sociology* 2(2): 132–143.

Reid, W. V., H. A. Mooney, A. Cropper, D. Capistrano, S. R. Carpenter, K. Chopra, & M. B. Zurek. (2005). *Ecosystems and Human Well-Being-Synthesis: A Report of the Millennium Ecosystem Assessment*. Washington, DC: Island Press.

Ripple, W. J., C. Wolf, T. M. Newsome, P. Barnard, & W. R. Moomaw. (2019). World scientists' warning of a climate emergency. *BioScience*. November 5.

Roberts, D. (2018). I'm an environmental journalist, but I never write about overpopulation. Here's why. *Vox*. November 29, 2018. https://www.vox.com/energy-and-environment/2017/9/26/16356524/the-population-question

Roberts, J. T., & B. Parks. (2006). *A Climate of Injustice: Global Inequality, North-South Politics, and Climate Policy*. Cambridge, MA: MIT Press.

Roberts, J. T., J. K. Steinberger, T. Dietz, W. F. Lamb, R. York, A. K. Jorgenson, J. E. Givens, P. Baer, & J. B. Schor. (2020). Four agendas for research and policy on emissions mitigation and well-being. *Global Sustainability* 3.

Romano, O. (2012). How to rebuild democracy, re-thinking degrowth. *Futures* 44(6): 582–589.

Rosnick, D. (2013). Reduced work hours as a means of slowing climate change. *Real-World Economic Review* 63: 124–133.

Rosnick, D., & M. Weisbrot. (2006). Are shorter working hours good for the environment? A comparison of U.S. and European Energy consumption. Washington, DC: Center for Economic and Policy Research.

Rudel, T. K., R. Defries, G. P. Asner, & W. F. Laurance. (2009). Changing drivers of deforestation and new opportunities for conservation. *Conservation Biology* 23(6): 1396–1405.

Rudel, T. K. (2016). Land use and the great acceleration in human activities. In G. Hooks (ed.) *The Sociology of Development Handbook* (pp. 190–206). Berkeley: University of California Press.

Santarius, T. (2012). Green growth unraveled: How rebound effects baffle sustainability targets when the economy keeps growing. Wuppertal Institute, Berlin, Germany.

Sapinski, J. P. (2017). Sociological theorizing as meaning making: the case of ecological modernization theory. https://osf.io/5qthx/

Satheesh, S. (2020). Moving beyond class: A critical review of labor-environmental conflicts from the global south. *Sociology Compass:* e12797.

Scanu, E. (2015). Climate governance in the post-industrial city: The urban side of ecological modernisation. *Environmental Sociology* 1(2): 102–115.

Schifeling, T., & A. J. Hoffman. (2019). Bill McKibben's influence on US climate change discourse: shifting field-level debates through radical flank effects. *Organization & Environment* 32(3): 213–233.

Schlosberg, D. (2013). Theorising environmental justice: the expanding sphere of a discourse. *Environmental Politics* 22(1): 37–55.

Schlosberg, D., & D. Carruthers. (2010). Indigenous struggles, environmental justice, and community capabilities. *Global Environmental Politics* 10(4): 12–35.

Schlosberg, D., & L. B. Collins. (2014). From environmental to climate justice: climate change and the discourse of environmental justice. *Wiley Interdisciplinary Reviews: Climate Change* 5(3): 359–374.

Schnaiberg, A. (1980). *The Environment: From Surplus to Scarcity.* New York: Oxford University Press.

Schnaiberg, A., & K. A. Gould. (1994). *Environment and Society.* Caldwell, NJ: Blackburn Press.

Schor, J., & K. E. White. (2010). *Plenitude: The New Economics of True Wealth.* New York: Penguin Press.

Schor, J. B. (2014). *Born to Buy: The Commercialized Child and the New Consumer Cult.* New York: Simon and Schuster.

Schor, J. (2015). Climate, inequality, and the need for reframing climate policy. *Review of Radical Political Economics* 47(4): 525–536.

Schor, J. B. (2018). Consumption and social inequality. *Core Concepts in Sociology* 46.

Schor, J. B., & A. K. Jorgenson. (2019). Is it too late for growth? *Review of Radical Political Economics* 51(2): 320–329.

Simpson, J. M., R. E. Dunlap, & A. S. Fullerton. (2019). The Treadmill of Information: Development of the information society and carbon dioxide emissions. *Sociology of Development* 5(4): 381–409.

Smelser, N. J. (1962). *Theory of Collective Behavior.* New York: The Free Press.

Sol, J. (2019). Economics in the anthropocene: Species extinction or steady state economics. *Ecological Economics* 165: 06392.

Steffen, W., K. Richardson, J. Rockström, S. E. Cornell, I. Fetzer, E. M. Bennett, R. Biggs, S. R. Carpenter, W. De Vries, C. A. De Wit, & C. Folke. (2015). Planetary boundaries: guiding human development on a changing planet. *Science* 347(6223): 1259855.

Steffen, W., J. Rockström, K. Richardson, T. M. Lenton, C. Folke,

D. Liverman, & J. F. Donges. (2018). Trajectories of the Earth System in the Anthropocene. *Proceedings of the National Academy of Sciences* 115(33): 8252–8259.

Stern, P. C. (2000). Toward a coherent theory of environmentally significant behaviour. *Journal of Social Issues* 56(3): 407–424.

Stern, P. C., G. T. Gardner, M. P. Vandenbergh, T. Dietz, & J. M. Gilligan. (2010). Design principles for carbon emissions reduction programs. *Environmental Science and Technology*. https://pubs.acs.org/doi/abs/10.1021/es100896p

Stiglitz, J. E. (2009). The Great GDP Swindle. *The Guardian*. September 12.

Stiglitz, J. E. (2019a). *Measuring What Counts: The Global Movement for Well-Being*. New York: The New Press.

Stiglitz, J. E. (2019b). It's time to retire metrics like GDP. They don't measure everything that matters. *The Guardian*. November 24. https://www.theguardian.com/commentisfree/2019/nov/24/metrics-gdp-economic-performance-social-progress

Stoddart, M. C., T. Ylä-Anttila, & D. B. Tindall. (2017). Media, politics, and climate change: The ASA Task Force report and beyond. *Environmental Sociology* 3(4): 309–320.

Stuart, D., R. Gunderson, & B. Petersen. (2019). Climate change and the Polanyian counter-movement: Carbon markets or degrowth?. *New Political Economy* 24(1): 89–102.

Stuart, D., & R. Gunderson. (2020). Human-animal relations in the capitalocene: environmental impacts and alternatives. *Environmental Sociology* 6(1): 68–81.

Stuart, D., R. Gunderson, & B. Petersen. (2020). Overconsumption as ideology: Implications for addressing global climate change. *Nature and Culture* 15(2): 199–223.

Stuart, D., & M. Houser. (2018). Producing compliant polluters: Seed companies and nitrogen fertilizer application in U.S. corn agriculture. *Rural Sociology* 83(4): 857–881.

Taylor, D. (2014). *Toxic Communities: Environmental Racism, Industrial Pollution, and Residential Mobility*. New York: NYU Press.

Ternes, B. (2019). Saving for a dry day: Investigating well ownership and watering practices during droughts. *Environmental Sociology* 5(1): 93–107.

Therborn, G. (1980). *The Power of Ideology and the Ideology of Power*. London: Verso.

Tilly, C. (1978). *From Mobilization to Revolution*. New York: McGraw Hill.

Tufekci, Z. (2017). *Twitter and Tear Gas: The Power and Fragility of Networked Protest*. New Haven, CT: Yale University Press.

Vandenbergh, M. P., P. C. Stern, G. T. Gardner, T. Dietz, & J. M. Gilligan. (2010). Implementing the behavioral wedge: Designing and adopting effective carbon emissions reduction programs. *Environmental Laws and Reporter, News & Analysis* 40: 10547.

Veblen, Thorstein. (2005). *Conspicuous Consumption.* Harmondsworth: Penguin.

Vickery, J., & L. M. Hunter. (2014). Native Americans: Where in environmental justice theory and research? *Unpublished Population Health.* University of Colorado, Denver.

Vickery, J., H. Brenkert-Smith, & H. Qin. (2020). Using joint constitution to understand responses to slow-moving environmental change: the case of mountain pine beetle in north-central Colorado. *Environmental Sociology* 6(2): 182, 193.

Victor, P. A. (2010). Questioning economic growth. *Nature* 468(7322): 370–371

Wallace-Wells, D. (2019). *The Uninhabitable Earth: Life after Warming.* Tim Duggan Books.

Wallerstein, I. (1974). *The Modern World-System.* New York: Academic Press.

Werfel, S. H. (2017). Household behaviour crowds out support for climate change policy when sufficient progress is perceived. *Nature Climate Change* 7(7): 512–515.

Westoby, P., & K. Lyons. (2016). Privatising development and environmental management: undermining social license in the Ugandan plantation forest sector. *Environmental Sociology* 2(3): 265–274.

Wiedmann, T. O., H. Schandl, M. Lenzen, D. Moran, S. Suh, J. West, & K. Kanemoto. (2015). The material footprint of nations. *Proceedings of the National Academy of Sciences of the United States of America* 112(20): 6271–6276.

Wilson, S., R. Bullard, J. Patterson, & S. B. Thomas. (2020). Environmental Justice Roundtable on COVID-19. *Environmental Justice* 13(3): 56–64.

Wolske, K. S., P. C. Stern, & T. Dietz. (2017). Explaining interest in adopting residential solar photovoltaic systems in the United States: Toward an integration of behavioral theories. *Energy Research & Social Science* 25: 134–151.

Wright, E. O. (2010). *Envisioning real utopias* (Vol. 98). London: Verso.

Wright, E. O. (2019). *How To Be an Anticapitalist in the Twenty-first Century.* London: Verso.

York, R. (2012a). Asymmetric effects of economic growth and decline on CO_2 emissions. *Nature Climate Change* 2(11): 762–764.

York, R. (2012b). Do alternative energy sources displace fossil fuels? *Nature Climate Change* 2(6): 441–443.

York, R. (2017). Why petroleum did not save the whales. *Socius* 3: 1–13.

York, R., E. A. Rosa, & T. Dietz. (2002). Bridging environmental science with environmental policy: Plasticity of population, affluence, and technology. *Social Science Quarterly* 83(1): 18–34.

York, R., E. A. Rosa, & T. Dietz. (2003a). STIRPAT, IPAT and

ImPACT: Analytic tools for unpacking the driving forces of environmental impacts. *Ecological Economics* 46(3): 351–365.

York, R., E. A. Rosa, & T. Dietz. (2003b). A rift in modernity? Assessing the anthropogenic sources of global climate change with the STIRPAT model. *International Journal of Sociology and Social Policy* 84(3): 1798.

York, R., E. A. Rosa, & T. Dietz. (2009). A tale of contrasting trends: Three measures of the ecological footprint in China, India, Japan, and the United States, 1961–2003. *Journal of World-Systems Research* 15(2): 134–46.

York, R., & B. Clark. (2010). Critical materialism: science, technology, and environmental sustainability. *Sociological Inquiry* 80(3): 475–499.

York, R., E. A. Rosa, & T. Dietz. (2010). Ecological modernization theory: Theoretical and empirical challenges. *The International Handbook of Environmental Sociology*: 77–90.

York, R., C. Ergas, E. A. Rosa, & T. Dietz. (2011). It's a material world: Trends in material extraction in China, India, Indonesia, and Japan. *Nature and Culture* 6(2): 103–122.

York, R., & J. A. McGee. (2016). Understanding the Jevons paradox. *Environmental Sociology* 2(1): 77–87.

York, R., & S. E. Bell. (2019). Energy transitions or additions? Why a transition from fossil fuels requires more than the growth of renewable energy. *Energy Research & Social Science* 51: 40–43.

York, R., & Dunlap, R. E. (2019). Environmental sociology. *The Wiley Blackwell Companion to Sociology* (pp. 283–300). Hoboken, NJ: John Wiley & Sons.

Zinn, J. O. (2016). Living in the Anthropocene: Towards a risk-taking society. *Environmental Sociology* 2(4): 385–394.

Index